Endorsements

I have known Scott for 15 of the 20 years of the journey he describes in this amazing book. Scott is an authentic practitioner of the ongoing ministry of Jesus Christ and his kingdom, which easily flows through him to others around him. This was not always the case. In this book Scott describes the keys that he and everyday believers need to unlock the supernatural ministry of Jesus through them to the world around them. I have had firsthand testimony of these miracles, or was present for some of them that Scott unpacks in this book. I can attest that the result of the ministry he describes is genuine and with lasting effect. His walk and testimony have been an inspiration to me personally and many in our church and school of ministry over the years. There is significant impartation for you in the pages of this book. If you want to go deeper in the ministry of the kingdom of God, or perhaps unlock it for the first time, I implore you to read this book, soak in it, practice it, and you will soon find yourself with your own stories to tell. God is that good and there is a world to win! Enjoy the journey!

Peter Young
Senior Leader, BridgeWay Church Denver

As you read the stories in this book, you might be tempted to think of them as fabrications. They are not. I know the man, Scott Pearson. He carries an unusual joy and a unique perspective.

He absolutely believes God can do anything. I am also the recipient of healing through his prayers. Several years ago, I had a bicycle accident and injured my shoulder. I thought I had broken my collarbone, but after numerous X-rays, the doctors told me there was no breakage. Nevertheless, every time I lifted my arm above my shoulder, searing pain would seize my arm all the way down to my wrist. I was unable to play the guitar, a passion of mine, because of the pain. After two years of pain, I visited the healing room, where every Wednesday night, Scott and a few others pray for people's healing. After they prayed for me, Scott asked me to check my arm out. As I lifted my arm, there was still pain with no apparent change. However, the next morning, when I lifted my arm to squeegee the shower door, I noticed a difference. I braced for the pain, but I didn't feel a thing. I started lifting my arm repeatedly above my head and the pain was completely gone! That was two years ago. I was marvelously healed, and I celebrate my healing every day by practicing my guitar. So, as you read Scott's testimonies and the lessons he has learned, I hope you will be encouraged, as I have been, that God can and wants to do through us what He has been doing through Scott. God does not discriminate. He desires for each one of us to embrace our identity as sons and daughters and join with Him in the family business of spreading His redemptive love.

Steve Beard
Infor, Vice-President of Solution Consulting

God on the Move: Encountering the Love of God speaks to risk-taking and the love of God. Scott Pearson takes us through his journey of deep hunger for God, and a willingness to say yes to Him regardless of time and circumstance. The power of his testimony encourages us to say yes as well. An essential read perfect for such a time as this.

John Borman
Associate Professor, Colorado Christian University

I want to recommend this book *God on the Move: Encountering the Love of God* written by a close friend of mine, Scott Pearson. It is a book that Scott was destined to write as it describes his life and his walk with the Holy Spirit, Jesus, and God. Scott is a humble man and loves others deeply and warmly. Scott has seen the Holy Spirit show up and be an overflow of God's abundant love for each one of us individually. For many years as a devoted Christian, I did not believe God moved in supernatural ways today. A little over twenty years ago, my wife and kids all got very ill with Lyme disease. They were all so sick that both of my kids missed all of junior and high school unable to function at all. In 2012, after ten years of this misery and suffering, I saw God love us compassionately and heal my wife and children. This miraculous healing caused me to re-evaluate how I looked at the Bible where it describes the amazing supernatural working of the Holy Spirit. This book is Scott's journey with the Holy Spirit in seeing signs, wonders, and miracles in his life and others, and it can also be your journey. This book describes God's love and Scott lays for us a simple way and demonstrates the faith so that we can all see the Holy Spirit move in our lives and hear the voice of Jesus for ourselves. Step back and suspend your preconceived notions of how Jesus moves today and enjoy this book.

John G. Edwards, CGFM
Budget and Finance Manager

I have known Scott and his dear wife Lynea for over ten years. On each occasion that I am with them I always leave encouraged, refreshed and joyful. Scott lives these stories. He literally becomes a walking encounter with Jesus. I have been with him and prayed for people on a few occasions and both witnessed and been affected by his relationship with Jesus and the power he carries. I am thrilled to recommend this book to you! In it you will find many of the testimonies Scott has shared with me over coffee and fellowship, and many others. I also love the way he makes it simple and accessible for anyone to understand and move in the same kind of anointing that he does. Read this book, experiment with it, and most of all grow closer to Jesus in your adventure.

Doug Burroughs, Founder and Senior Leader
Fusion Ministries International

After reading this book, what more could we say to encourage you to follow Scott's example into the incredible adventure that is following Jesus, other than to tell you that Scott is the most normal, regular guy we know. He isn't some flashy personality that naturally garners attention in whatever room he finds himself in. He's just Scott. A normal guy from Colorado that just wants to see Jesus touch his city.

Alex & Natalie Malaska

God on the Move

Encountering God's Love

SCOTT AND LYNEA PEARSON

Copyright © 2022 Scott Pearson

ISBN Softcover: 979-8-88739-017-8
eBook ISBN: 979-8-88739-018-5

All rights reserved. No part of this book may be reproduced or transmitted in any form or by any means, electronic or mechanical, including photocopying, recording or by any information storage and retrieval system, without permission in writing from the copyright owner. For information on distribution rights, royalties, derivative works or licensing opportunities on behalf of this content or work, please contact the publisher at the address below.

Printed in the United States of America.

Cover Design: Zach Marrel

Although the author and publisher have made every effort to ensure that the information and advice in this book was correct and accurate at press time, the author and publisher do not assume and hereby disclaim any liability to any party for any loss, damage, or disruption caused from acting upon the information in this book or by errors or omissions, whether such errors or omissions result from negligence, accident, or any other cause.

Scripture taken from the New King James Version®. Copyright © 1982 by Thomas Nelson. Used by permission. All rights reserved.

Scriptures taken from the Holy Bible, New International Version®, NIV®. Copyright © 1973, 1978, 1984, 2011 by Biblica, Inc.™ Used by permission of Zondervan. All rights reserved worldwide. www.zondervan.com The "NIV" and "New International Version" are trademarks registered in the United States Patent and Trademark Office by Biblica, Inc.™

Scripture quotations marked TPT are from The Passion Translation®. Copyright © 2017, 2018, 2020 by Passion & Fire Ministries, Inc. Used by permission. All rights reserved. ThePassionTranslation.com.

Throne Publishing
1601 E 69th St #306
Sioux Falls, SD 57108

Dedication

To our children, Hannah and John.

We dedicate our first book to you.

Thank you for listening to Dad's stories and joining us in this journey.

We love you!

Acknowledgements

To Dad and Mom, thank you for believing
and investing in us and the book.

To Chris Tracy, you are an amazing editor,
and we couldn't have written this book
without your encouragement and belief in us.

To Natalie Malaska, thank you for taking time
in your busy schedule to do a thorough edit.
You are skilled at wordsmithing!

Table of Contents

Introduction . . . . *xiii*

CHAPTER 1:   It Began at McDonald's 1
CHAPTER 2:   In Spite of 11
CHAPTER 3:   My Mall 19
CHAPTER 4:   Rest 29
CHAPTER 5:   Timing is Everything 37
CHAPTER 6:   Is Your Name Al? 47
CHAPTER 7:   Manna from Heaven 57
CHAPTER 8:   Want to Have Some Fun? 65
CHAPTER 9:   Identity 77
CHAPTER 10:   Holy Spirit 85
CHAPTER 11:   Hearing and Awareness 105
CHAPTER 12:   Believing and Acting 111

Conclusion *117*
About the Authors *121*

Introduction

God is doing signs, wonders, and miracles every minute of every day. As His children, we have an open invitation to join Him as He touches people with His love. How? Through supernatural living. This book chronicles my supernatural encounters and amazing experiences with God over the past twenty years. It has been an incredible journey during which I have learned much and made lots of mistakes along the way.

> ## "WE HAVE AN OPEN INVITATION TO JOIN HIM"

Many are hungry to walk in the events of Acts but find themselves plagued with fear. Indeed, one of our greatest challenges as human beings is to walk daily with the Holy Spirit, hearing His voice, and stepping out to share God's love with others. As I can personally attest, the key is to remember that God is "not a respecter of persons" – and part of my mission is to help you do the same.

Christians today have the same questions I had, and the same desire to step into a supernatural lifestyle that shows and looks like the biblical examples we've been given. My hope is that this book will feed that hunger so you will pursue God and begin to walk in signs, wonders and miracles on a daily basis. To join with

God is to release the kingdom of God, and there is no greater joy than to see people set free, delivered, healed, saved, encouraged, and built up.

I am extending the invitation to join in the adventure and see people's lives radically changed.

CHAPTER 1

IT BEGAN AT MCDONALD'S

"We have a God who delights in impossibilities."
– Billy Sunday

MY FIRST BRUSH WITH THE SUPERNATURAL
Denver, Colorado

For most of my life I have been on a journey with the Lord and hungry for God to move in people's lives in mighty ways. I first saw evidence of this as an elementary school-age child in the early 1970s, when I was invited to attend church with a friend. I attended church regularly with my family, but this service was going to be different. Kathryn Kuhlman, a healing evangelist who wore long white dresses, was scheduled to speak.

When we went into the church, I noticed they had taken out a huge portion of seating on one side to make room for thirty wheelchairs. As the service started, Kathryn began to talk about how much Jesus loves people and one of the ways He demonstrates His love is through healing. She then stopped in the middle of her preaching and made a comment that caught me off guard: Jesus was coming to the service to heal people. That was totally new to me, and I didn't know what to expect.

Suddenly, something in the church began to change; I could actually feel it in the air around me. Kathryn said again that Jesus was coming to heal, but this time she referred specifically to the people in the wheelchairs. Sure enough, over the next ten to fifteen minutes, a dozen people got up out of their wheelchairs – they had been healed! I stared, awestruck, knowing even at that young age that I would never forget the experience as long as I lived. It planted a seed in my heart that continued to grow as I did.

WORDS OF KNOWLEDGE

During my sophomore year in high school, I was invited to an event held by the Vineyard Movement – a charismatic evangelical denomination founded by John Wimber in the 1970s. I was very excited about this, as Daniels was a world-famous Christian musician and worship leader who had been working and traveling with John Wimber for decades.

"My heart was stirred"

At the event, people were sharing words of knowledge about what others were experiencing in their physical bodies. A word of knowledge is the ability to know what God is currently doing or intends to do in a person's life.

In this case, the words of knowledge concerned illness, injury, or trauma in a person's physical body. For example, someone would call out a particular disease or ailment, then people with that ailment would come to the front for prayer, and God would touch them. Those who had been healed of what was called out in the word of knowledge would testify to that fact. Again, my heart was stirred, and another seed was planted.

Throughout high school and college, I read everything I could get my hands on about God's generals who did signs and wonders.

My personal favorites were Smith Wigglesworth, a British evangelist who moved in healing, signs, and wonders in the late 1800s and William Seymour, who led the Azusa Street Revival in Los Angeles, California from 1906 to 1915.

MIRACLES IN ZIMBABWE

My next, and most impactful, experience witnessing the supernatural began with a conversation with a pastor friend. By this time, I was a young man in my early twenties, married and in Bible college preparing to plant a church in our city. One day I was speaking with my friend, and I wondered why we don't see God move supernaturally around us. He suggested that I meet Ezekiel Guti, an apostle who lived in Zimbabwe and had a movement for God in that part of the world.

In the summer of 1993, my wife and I led a mission trip to Zimbabwe. Neither of us had traveled overseas or led a mission trip, but that didn't stop us. We were so hungry for the things of God and what He was doing in the world.

In Africa, two things happened that changed everything for me. First, Dr. Guti anointed and ordained me to minister in his churches. In order to be a pastor in his ministry, one had to have three qualifications: the ability to preach the gospel (message of salvation through Jesus Christ and the Kingdom of God), heal the sick, and deliver people from demons. In his office, Dr. Guti had me get on my knees and then he laid hands on me. I felt electricity run through my body and sensed a new anointing along with a power transfer. It took me a while to stand up afterwards. I had limited experience with healing and deliverance prior, and I experienced a huge change afterwards. It was one of the defining moments in my life and left me forever changed.

At the very first meeting I went to after I was anointed, I had an opportunity to preach and, at the end of the service, minister to those who were sick or wanted to be saved. The first person I prayed for was a lady who was completely blind – her eyes were white and had no pupils. I didn't know exactly what to do, so I laid my hands on her, said some simple words that included "In Jesus' Name be healed." Words cannot describe my complete and utter amazement as I watched eyes form in the lady's eye sockets. And she could see! Everyone in the meeting knew who she was and confirmed that she had been blind since birth. I was probably more shocked than she was. That was the first time the Lord used my hands and my obedience to manifest a miracle.

We continued to see amazing signs and wonders throughout our month in Africa. Every place we went, we saw people healed. We saw tumors disappear, blind eyes open, deaf ears open, and people who had been oppressed by demonic spirits delivered. We saw backs and headaches healed (the people there carry things on their heads). We saw people who had crippled arms and leprosy healed. God demonstrated His love through signs and wonders, and people saw that He was more powerful than other spirits who held them in fear. Once they had experienced God's love, they were open to the gospel of Jesus and became His followers.

In our travels, we saw a newspaper clipping about a local elder raised from the dead two days before we arrived in Karoi, Zimbabwe. Despite all I had experienced, hearing about this was surreal, let alone seeing it in a newspaper! When we got there and spoke to some of the locals, we learned that such phenomena were normal and happened all the time. At every meeting, every church service, and every event we were a part of, people were healed, delivered, saved, and set free of things they had been under their entire lives. It was absolutely mind-blowing.

Back home, I would share what God had done, and most believers quickly dismissed what had happened, saying that those things "only happen in Africa." This grieved my heart. I knew the God I served was the same and could do signs and wonders anywhere, and I started asking Him why this wasn't happening. It was the beginning of a new mission for me, to see people in the United States touched by God's love in a tangible way that would change their lives.

MIRACLE AT MCDONALD'S

In 1994, I planted a church in Lafayette, Colorado (east of Boulder, CO) and pastored the same church until 2021. I currently pastor the Bridgeway House Churches. I continued to pursue the supernatural and divine encounters and infrequently saw things happen.

Flash forward to a hot summer day in 2003, nearly ten years after that trip to Zimbabwe. In preparation for my sermon that coming Sunday, I was reading in Acts 8 about the story of the Ethiopian Eunuch and his interaction with Philip, the deacon of the church. I continued reading how the miracles happening in the area caused the fame and the testimony of Jesus to spread throughout that city.

"When the crowds heard Philip and saw the miraculous signs he did, they all paid close attention to what he said. With shrieks, evil spirits came out of many, and many paralytics and cripples were healed. So there was great joy in that city." (Acts 8: 6–8 (NIV))

The phrase "great joy in the city" jumped out at me. It was a joy born of witnessing Jesus' miracles and talking about them with each other. I thought about the numerous trips I had been on over the last decade, all the amazing healings I had seen, not just individually but in whole towns and villages touched by God and the gospel. And that's when the realization hit me like a ton of bricks.

I didn't want to go on talking about what had happened in the past. I wanted to see it in my city today, here and now. I wanted people in *my* streets talking about what Jesus had done, about the miracles of people being healed, people being saved, people being set free.

Suddenly, I began to weep. "I can't do this," I said. "I can't keep talking to people about these happenings all over the world, when they are not seeing them for themselves. I need you, Lord, to move me to do whatever is necessary. Show me what needs to happen so that I can see that through my own hands, see that in my own city, see that in the church." I then slammed my Bible shut, adding, "Until this happens, I'm not going to talk about this kind of stuff anymore."

For while I sat there, staring out the window, in this weird place of being frustrated yet knowing God wanted to move and that I could trust Him. A rumbling stomach interrupted my musings, and with a glance at the clock, I realized it was approaching lunchtime. Thinking nothing was going to be resolved in that moment, I got in the car and headed to McDonald's.

As I stood in line waiting to place my order, I noticed that the young man behind the counter – his name tag read Dave – didn't look very happy. Dave's mouth was pulled into a tight frown, and he was moving gingerly, as if he were in pain.

When it was my turn to come up to the counter, I asked Dave if he was okay. He told me he'd bruised a rib while playing basketball with some friends and was in terrible pain every time he took a breath or lifted something – any time he moved at all. *Was this the opportunity I had been asking for?* I didn't know, but it certainly seemed like an invitation. I asked Dave if I could pray for Jesus to heal that bruised rib and take away the pain. Dave looked at me kind of funny, then asked if I could pray for him right there in the middle of the lunch rush! I asked if he had a break coming up, to which he replied five minutes, so I ordered my food and told him where to find me.

I went to my table and waited, with no idea whether Dave was really going to show up, and what, if anything, would happen if he did. Sure enough, about five minutes later, there he was, lowering himself into the seat across from me. I said a short prayer, declaring the goodness of God over his body, spoke to the bruised rips to be healed, and asked for the pain to leave. As I was praying, I noticed a change in his face – like there was *something* going on. I asked him about it, and he reported that he was feeling heat in his body. "Well, that's good," I replied. "Heat is good. Let's continue to pray."

After about two minutes of prayer, the heat left, and with it, the pain! I asked him to move around and do some things that he couldn't do before. A huge smile spread across Dave's face as he confirmed that the pain had simply vanished. The Lord had totally healed his bruised rib! I then began to talk to him about how much Jesus cared about him, and how other people would be encouraged to hear about what God had just done. When Dave told me that he was Catholic, a denomination I knew also believed in miracles, I asked if he be willing to share this experience with his priest. He agreed and returned to work a changed young man. I was willing to bet that change went beyond the physical.

I went back my lunch, barely noticing that it had gone cold; I was too busy enjoying the presence of the Lord and marveling at what He had done. Less than an hour before I had pleaded with Him to show His presence in my community, and now Jesus had healed this kid at – of all places – a McDonald's right down the street from my work!

Little did I know the Lord and I had an audience.

A few minutes later, an older woman came up to my table. She had been watching me and Dave and wanted to know what had happened. I told the story of Dave's bruised ribs and how as we were praying God touched him and healed his ribs.

"Yeah, that's what I thought I heard," she said, her eyes darting to a table behind me. "I was wondering if you'd be willing to pray for my husband."

I turned around and there sat a man with a tube in his nose; a portable oxygen machine sat on the floor beside him. The woman told me his name was Neil, and he had been on oxygen since suffering a heart attack. My mind reeling that this was happening for a second time, I went over and introduced myself to Neil. I then laid my hand on his shoulder and asked the Lord to heal his heart and lungs so he would have plenty of oxygen without the tank.

I could tell Neil was receiving the prayer; I also noticed his face was kind of *red*. When I asked if he was okay, he replied, "Wow, I'm feeling something … I've never felt this before."

"I think that's God healing you."

I continued to pray, first in English then in the spirit, for a few more minutes until I felt the Holy Spirit was done.

"How do we know," I asked, "whether or not something has happened here? Would you have to go to the doctor to get a checkup? Or what would happen?"

"Well, if I shut off this machine, I'll know in about ten to fifteen minutes because my lips will start turning blue and it will be obvious that I'm not getting enough oxygen."

I stepped out and asked if he would be willing to turn off his oxygen.

"Sure," he said, already reaching down toward the machine, "I'll do that."

THINGS HAPPEN IN THREES

I went back to my seat and started eating again, nearly bursting with excitement. Two people in ten minutes? God was certainly doing some miraculous things right here! That's when I felt like someone was staring at me and looked over. It was two people, actually, an older lady and a younger one, sitting at a table nearby. They were looking at me kind of funny, and I was pretty sure they'd seen what happened with Neil. I also had a feeling the Lord was creating another opportunity, so I went over to their table, said hello, and introduced myself.

"I STEPPED OUT"

Just as the older woman expressed her curiosity about what had been going on, I spotted Dave cleaning some tables nearby and asked if he could share what happened. He didn't hesitate; he just came right over and recounted the whole story for them. I could tell by the looks on the women's faces that they didn't know what to do with it. I then shared that God had also given me the opportunity to pray for Neil, God touched him during that prayer, and now we were waiting to see how he did without his oxygen. Noting the questioning look on the younger woman's face, I started to talk about how Jesus loves people and that He heals and is still healing today. I told them healing is a demonstration of His love for us and that He is inviting people to be in relationship with Him.

The young lady looked across the table. "Yeah, my mom has been praying for a long time that I would accept Jesus, and I've just really had no desire to do that. But sitting here today listening to this, maybe I do. Maybe I really want to accept Jesus. Maybe I want to give my life to Him."

And, after I'd shared the gospel with her and answered her questions, that's exactly what she did! She had a big smile on her face, and her mother was crying tears of joy that she'd been saved. We were celebrating a new sister in the kingdom.

Suddenly, I felt this hand on my shoulder and turned to find Neil's wife standing there. It had been twenty minutes since he'd shut off the oxygen, and he was perfectly fine. I looked over at Neil's smiling face and knew God had completely healed him of whatever was causing him to need oxygen. I was overwhelmed by God's goodness and how He'd demonstrated His love to those around me. What an amazing day at McDonald's!

I went back over to my seat and picked up the cold remains of my lunch. *Wow*, I thought, *this is what it should be like. This is what I was made for, to be a steward of the Kingdom of God, doing what Jesus said His followers would do, sharing God's love and goodness.* It made me think of the passage from the book of Matthew when Jesus sent out His disciples, instructing them: "As you go, proclaim this message. The Kingdom of Heaven has come near. Heal the sick, raise the dead, cleanse those that have leprosy, drive out demons. Freely you have received, freely give." (Matthew 10: 7–8 (NIV))

Sitting in that McDonald's, I'd had an opportunity to do some of those things. Two people were healed, a young lady committed her life to Jesus, and a mom saw her prayers answered. I decided that day to allow myself to be led by the Holy Spirit like never before. I needed to see God moving through me. I needed to hear His voice. I needed to respond to His voice. I need to recognize what's going on around me so that I can engage and see the Kingdom of God advancing. I was no longer willing to accept anything less.

This was a pivotal moment, one that would change my life forever. I'd been a minister for a long time. I had read the Scriptures. I had seen God's amazing work around the world and dreamed about being His conduit for healing in my city. I had gone to conferences about how to do it. But when God showed up at lunch that day, He'd given me my first opportunity to do it right here in the

United States, not in some mission field, not in some church service. As the Apostle Peter said, God is "no respecter of people," and He can do the same thing in your life and in your neighborhood. (Acts 10:34 (NIV))

QUESTIONS:

1. What has been your journey with the Lord and the supernatural?
2. Reflect on Matthew 10: 7–8.
3. Jesus taught His disciples to pray, "Your kingdom come, Your will be done on earth as it is in heaven." What does that mean to you?

CHAPTER 2

IN SPITE OF...

*"Remembering the goodness of God in the past,
will help us in seasons where it's harder to see Him."
– Esther Fleece*

In 2003, my journey in praying for people started, and I have learned much – and have had many struggles – since then. You may be thinking everyone I pray for gets healed, and to this I say, "Not yet." Do people receive what God is doing every time? The answer is no. Do I see miracles and signs and wonders every time I step out? Again, not yet. Does it stop me from praying for people or stepping out? Absolutely not! Over the years, I have prayed for thousands of people, and some have been healed and some have not. No doubt you're wondering why. It is something I have wondered myself, and here is what I've learned ...

GOD IS GOOD

God is good all the time, and His desire is to see people healed, delivered, and set free. When you don't see something happen, that does not change the fact that God is good or that He wants to demonstrate His love for people. That is what happens when we pray for people: We are allowing ourselves to be a conduit for His love.

I believe the primary reason we don't see something happen every time we pray is that we live in a fallen world. We are in a real spiritual war. As it says in 2 Corinthians 10:4 (NIV), "The weapons we fight with are not the weapons of the world. On the contrary, they have divine power to demolish strongholds." Every day we choose who we are going to align with. I have chosen to believe in the One who has overcome the power of the enemy. His name is Jesus Christ, and He's the one we believe in, trust in, and agree with when He says, "The thief comes only to steal and kill and destroy; I have come that they may have life, and have it to the full." (John 10:10 (NIV))

> "When you don't see something happen, that does not change the fact that God is good"

We live in a paradox, one in which we know that God wants everyone to be saved, set free and healed and do not always see that happen. As someone who has a daughter with cerebral palsy, I live with this paradox every day. Over the years, God has touched her and made her life better, but we have yet to see her completely healed. I have prayed for her literally thousands of times, other people have prayed for her, and she has experienced some degree of healing. However, she still lives with the effects of the stroke she had in utero, seizures, and mild cognitive impairment – as well as the effects of seventeen surgeries and other related disabilities.

On a related note, I was part of a team that prayed and saw two children with Down syndrome totally healed in Thailand. I've also prayed for dozens of people who had cancer and were healed, while my own mom died from cancer of the pancreas.

It is natural to want to ask the Lord why. The disciples did, for example, when they asked why Jesus taught in parables (Matthew 13:10). I have found, however, that if I stay in that space too long, I get discouraged, depressed, and hopeless. I have learned to lay my questions down at His feet, remember His goodness, and put the questions on a shelf to ask when I see Him in Heaven. When I shift my gaze back to Him, my heart is encouraged, and I am able to move on. I put my focus and awareness on God Himself, what He has promised, and what He has accomplished. No matter what is going on around me, I have an anchor that is attached to something that is absolutely consistent and absolutely true. God is completely dependable and completely good.

There are times you pray once before you see something happen, other times you pray twice or multiple times. The point is, by being persistent and consistent in stepping out and following the voice of the Lord, you *will* see miracles. Again, you won't necessarily see it all the time. Sometimes the healing takes place after we've left, overnight, or over time. I hand out cards with my name and number to people after I pray for them and ask them to call when something happens. I'm always filled with joy when my phone rings and it's someone wanting to share the fullness of all God has done.

It's always challenging when we don't know the final outcome. The key is to focus on our part – to step out, pray, and have an expectation that God wants to and does perform miracles every day. Sometimes we are just one piece of the puzzle. We may be one of many who pray and then finally, it breaks through, and the healing or miracle manifests itself. (1 Corinthians 3:6–9) My focus is not on whether there's a healing or not. My focus isn't on the miracles. My focus isn't on the outcome. My focus is on God Himself, and my desire to do what He wants me to do. This is why I am moved to continue, regardless of any outcome I can perceive in the natural.

My desire is also to share God's love with others. Jesus said He did only what He saw the Father doing. He said only what He heard the Father say. When I hear Him or sense Him leading me in a direction, I step out in obedience and respond. There are times I miss it and that is okay. There are times that nothing happens, and that is okay too. Success is not whether the healing occurs. Success is that I have responded to God's leading, took a risk, and loved the person in front of me.

Sometimes I pray for people and don't see anything happening in the physical, but they'll thank me over and over again for my willingness to recognize what was going on and bring God into the situation. Those encounters are just as amazing to me as seeing them healed. They were encouraged that someone "saw" them and showed them God's love. I get the privilege of being God's hands and feet.

Another thing I always try to keep in mind is that when I have my focus on Him, I am far more likely to hear His requests and carry them out.

Over the past twenty years, I have found three keys to keep me focused on the Lord as I pray for people, rather than the results visible to my human eyes.

KEEPING MY EYES ON WHO GOD IS

The first thing I do is keep my eyes on God and what He has promised. I remind myself that although it appears nothing has happened, God is still good; He loves people and wants to heal them. Healing is part of the promise and the finished work of Christ ("… And by His stripes, we are healed." Isaiah 53:5 (NKJV)). God is still healing today. I remind myself that these things are true; I read the Scriptures specifically connected to those promises to remind myself who He is. I begin to feast on the truth and "I remain confident of this: I will see the goodness of the Lord in the land of the living." (Psalm 27:13 (NIV))

TESTIMONIES

The Bible talks about remembering the things that God has done. (Psalm 77:11 (NIV)) The second thing I do is spend time remembering the things the Lord has done in my own life. I write them down so I can go back and refer to them. I use the testimonies often to encourage myself by speaking them out loud, rehearsing them in my mind, and declaring that they can happen again.

These testimonies are not only about things I personally experienced or witnessed; they also come from a variety of sources, including direct accounts from others or miracles I have read about. Revelations 19:10b says, "For it is the Spirit of prophecy who bears testimony to Jesus." (NIV) If someone has seen a miracle happen, anyone can see the same miracles happen. If I don't have a personal testimony about a specific situation like healing ADHD, I'll take somebody else's testimony. I'll continue to remember that testimony, listen to it, think about it, and speak it aloud as though it was my own.

I also read testimonies of what Jesus did in the Bible, as well as testimonies revivalists have shared on church websites or newsletters. I remind myself that Jesus promised I will do the same things that He did and even greater things.

I take Him at His word.

I will also build myself up by saying, "I can do it again. I can risk again. I'm going to hear God's voice to do this again. I am not going to give up, and I'll overcome the challenge and any feelings of defeat." Declarations and reminding myself of all God has done are key for me to press through any fear and discouragement.

This book is full of testimonies of what God has done. Until you have your own testimonies, feel free to read these over and over again to build your faith and remind yourself of God's goodness.

PROMISES OF GOD

The third and final thing I do to encourage myself is read God's promises in the Scriptures. I have a list of favorites that I bring with me everywhere I go. Speaking them out loud helps me continue to step out and share God's goodness through praying for people.

Acts 10: 38 (NIV) states "… how God anointed Jesus of Nazareth with the Holy Spirit and power, and how He went around doing good and healing all who are under the power of the devil, because God was with him." Every time I read this Scripture I am reminded of Jesus' anointing and all He did to heal those around Him. The good news is that God has promised us that we will do the same things. Jesus promised the gift of the Holy Spirit and power. He is the agent. He is God Himself within us, and that's why we see amazing signs and wonders. He touches people's lives to demonstrate His love for them and draw them to Himself.

Jesus sent out His disciples, telling them to heal the sick and preach the kingdom of God. I believe the commission God has given us as believers. That is my desire, to do what Jesus said we would do as believers and followers of God. He said, "Very truly I tell you, whoever believes in Me will do the work that I have been doing, and they will do even greater things than these, because I am going to the Father." (John 14:12 (NIV)) Not surprisingly, I often spend time meditating on this specific promise.

I love that Scripture where He says, "But seek first His kingdom and all these things shall be given to you as well." (Matthew 6:33 (NIV)) The kingdom looks like love, encouragement, healing, signs, wonders, and people being set free.

"IT'S BEEN AN AWE-FILLED JOURNEY"

When you have challenging days, when you pray for multiple people and it appears nothing happened, remind yourself of the goodness of God. If you don't pray, you don't get to participate with the Lord in seeing people healed, delivered, and set free. Again, I am successful just by stepping out. If one person in a hundred is healed, it is worth it. One person is important to God, so that one person is important to me.

I have heard people say that healing is not as important as being born again and going to heaven. I agree that salvation is a big deal; however, I also know that healing is a big deal to the person who is sick. In my experience, people's hearts are more open to hear the gospel when they've experienced God's love through healing. We are the hands and feet of Jesus.

In the next section, I will share some of my divine encounters, when I was able to join the Lord in ministering to people. It's been an awe-filled journey, and one in which I have learned many things through trial and error. In the beginning, I talked about the one testimony I had over and over again until another divine encounter happened. Now I share what is fresh and current while still remembering what God has done. These testimonies can be used to encourage you to step out. Read them over, again and again as you start your own journey.

QUESTIONS:

1. What are the three ways you can encourage yourself when you don't see healing, signs, and wonders?
2. Reflect on Rahab's life in Joshua 2:9–13. How did God use Rahab? If He can use Rahab, can He use you?
3. How have you encouraged yourself in the Lord? Do you have personal prophecies written down in a place you can review them? Do you have testimonies you can review?

My Mall

"If you want to see God move, make a move."
– Mark Batterson

GOD IN ME

Since that day in McDonald's, I had been learning how to be aware of people around me and pray for them as opportunities arose. Two years later, I heard a message by a pastor in California. This particular sermon was about impacting the world around you by carrying God's presence within and loving your city. The pastor had adopted a store to bless, and whenever he was in the store, he prayed that God would increase the business and bring them prosperity. He would walk up and down the aisles, praying and releasing the kingdom of God and God's presence in the store. I was stirred by the testimony and the fact that the Holy Spirit is in me and rests upon me; therefore, where I go, I change the environment around me. That is the Holy Spirit at work.

Over time, he began to see numerous divine encounters and events that happened in the store, as did the previously skeptical store owner who reported that business picked up and the atmosphere changed. Hearing this, I thought, *"I could adopt a store too."*

This would be, and has been, a practical step to reaching my community with the love of God.

Wherever Jesus went, He brought the New Covenant, instead of letting the environment (Old Covenant) influence Him. Under the Old Covenant, if you came into contact with a leper or an adulterer, you became unclean. (Leviticus 13:1–3 (NIV)) In the New Covenant, however, the believer impacts those around them because we carry the presence of God. God *within us* changes the environment.

Jesus went to the houses of sinners, tax collectors, and leper colonies, but instead of becoming stained and infected by the sin in their lives, He was moved to heal, restore, and bring His kingdom into their lives, thus impacting *them.*

In the New Covenant, we are all filled with the Holy Spirit and are ambassadors for God's Kingdom everywhere we go. We are the influencers, not impacted by the world or those around us. We change the world and the situations all around us, so that others can experience who God is and see the Kingdom of God advance. The Holy Spirit, God Himself, lives within us and rests on us.

> "The Holy Spirit, God Himself, lives within us and rests on us"

STEPPING OUT

I began to ask God to teach me how to impact the environment around me and influence situations that were going on just by being in a room, store, person's house, or wherever else. I asked the Lord, "Where do you want me to change the environment in my own city?" I also shared my desire to partner with Him and have an impact for the Kingdom. I wanted to see someplace altered because I was there. I wanted to carry the Holy Spirit with me as an agent of change in each place.

I decided to adopt my local mall. I started by walking through the mall, going in and out of stores praying. After some time, I started introducing myself to people I saw regularly, including store workers and security guards. I let them know I was praying over the mall so they knew I was not some kind of weirdo stalking people. Over time I built relationships with these people.

Before I knew it, I was going several times a week and referring to it as "my mall." I had the mindset that I have authority in this place and I was bringing the kingdom of God to the mall. With every opportunity I had, I was consciously and purposely representing the Kingdom.

For the first several months, I felt that not much was happening. I had lots of conversations with different people, but no healings or miracles. On the other hand, I did notice vacant stores began to be filled, which encouraged me.

THE BEGINNING

One day, I was near the food court and noticed two middle-aged men eating their lunch. The Holy Spirit highlighted one of the men to me, so I went up and started talking to him. The Lord gave me a word of knowledge that the man had a hearing loss, so I asked him about it.

The man explained that he had been in the military, and as a result of being around loud sounds, he had lost a particular range and frequency in his hearing. His right ear had significant hearing loss, over eighty percent. When I asked if he'd be open to me praying for his ears to be healed, he excitedly said yes, adding that he was a believer. Not knowing what would happen, I stepped out in faith and laid hands on him. As I was praying, we both heard a loud pop and the man reported that he could hear clearly out of the right ear! Seeing my own excitement mirrored on his face, I then prayed over the other ear, which also had partial hearing and, sure enough, God opened that one as well.

As we talked and celebrated what God had done, the other man shared that he had a torn rotator cuff and was going to have to have shoulder surgery in the weeks ahead. Would I be willing to pray for his shoulder as well? I did, and God touched him, healing his rotator cuff. Within minutes, he was swinging his arm around in circles, something he was unable to do prior to the prayer, his face shining with the joy of a child!

We continued to chat about the miracle God had just brought, drawing the attention of one of the security guards who came by to make sure that I was not bothering these men. We told him about the healings, and though he was not a believer and did not know quite what to do with what he was hearing, he smiled, happy for the two men.

After this divine appointment, I continued my prayer course, filled with a new excitement about what God had done and already anticipating what He would do in the days ahead.

I was getting short on time that day, so I decided to finish my prayer route quickly. As I was walking around and going through stores, I noticed in my peripheral vision a young man in his teens, dressed in all black, following about fifty to a hundred feet behind me. Finally, I asked the Lord if I needed to stop and talk with him. I had the sense that I needed to continue what I was doing, so I finished my route, the young man following me the whole time. Then, as I was heading through a particular store toward the exit, the Lord indicated that I could stop. He was setting up a diving encounter.

THE MAN IN BLACK

I was in between the two sets of exit doors when I saw the young man again. I said, "Hey, I noticed you were kind of following me around. Is there something I can do for you?" He said he'd been standing nearby when I prayed for the men at the food court. Had he heard correctly, he asked, that one of the men had been healed of hearing loss when I prayed for him? Nodding, I shared the testimony with him.

The young man told me that while in a mosh pit at a concert, he'd been knocked over and kicked in the right temple area by someone wearing steel-toed boots. As a result of this injury, he lost all hearing in that ear. Could I pray for him too, he asked. I said, of course, and there, in the entryway of the mall, the Holy Spirit showed up again, in power. The young man could hear perfectly! Excited and praising God, he shared that he had been to a church in the area but had never really given his life to the Lord. He did so now, committing his life to Jesus because he felt God's love and experienced His healing touch. We exchanged information and parted ways, knowing we would see each other again.

PERSPECTIVE

This young man made a comment that has served as a major catalyst in my life, reminding me to always listen to God's voice and take advantage of the opportunities He gives me. "I grew up in the church," he said, "and I always thought that if there was a God, He would do things like this (miracles)." Over the years and after countless prayers for people, I've learned that many think this way, that if God is real and loves people, they should see Him move in supernatural ways and see miracles. They want to see Him demonstrate His love and that He is God. Love looks like something. People need to know that God is actively engaged in pursuing them.

> *"I always thought that if there was a God, He would do things like this (miracles)."*

THE STORY CONTINUES

I was thrilled when the young man and his family invited me over for dinner. As we ate, they told me about their lives, including the fact that the young man's sister, who lived in Los Angeles, had been physically assaulted and still suffered from severe emotional scarring. Fearful and unable to interact with people in public, she left her home only to go to work. She had even closed herself off to family and others who cared for her. She was, however, coming for a visit in a few weeks, and my new friends wanted to know if I could pray for her. The young man wondered aloud if I could do it any time. We talked about how God wants to heal and set people free, and I said I was willing to pray and believed God would touch his sister. We came up with a plan for us to meet at my mall. The family wanted it to appear natural, like it had just "happened."

At the prearranged date and time, I headed for the mall and "ran into" the family. Even before I was introduced to the sister, I sensed she was gripped with fear from the traumatic physical attack and demonically oppressed. During the conversation, we told her the testimony how God healed her brother's hearing. She didn't show any emotion after hearing the testimony. As we spoke, God gave me a word that He wanted to heal her by taking away her trauma and fear. He wanted to set her free.

Amazingly, she was open! Based on her history, I was surprised she said yes to a male stranger praying for her. I prayed for her right there in the mall. She began to manifest a demonic spirit, instantly dropping to the ground and making noises. I had seen similar demonic manifestations overseas in Africa and Thailand. When I first experienced a demon manifesting, I was a bit freaked out. Since I had experienced it multiple times, I was not scared by the manifestation and recognized what needed to happen to minister to her. People were walking by, staring and whispering and wondering what was going on. The security guard, I had interacted with multiple times before and was the one who saw the two men get healed earlier, noticed but didn't The same security guard I'd interacted with before, who'd seen the two men get healed, noticed but didn't interrupt. I quickly took authority over the demonic spirit and cast it out, and in the space of about thirty seconds we saw her get delivered from the evil spirit that had oppressed her since her attack. The young woman began to weep and was soon joined by her parents and brother. As the tears flowed, her family and I could see God heal and restore her – a radical and instantaneous change! I found out later that it was the first time she'd cried since the traumatic event because she'd been so emotionally shut down. I celebrated with the family, honored beyond words to be a part of sharing God's love and freedom.

As I was about to leave, a woman stopped me and asked if I could do that at any time. She then revealed that she was a clinical psychologist and worked with people who suffered from the effects of trauma. She believed they too were oppressed by demonic spirits – which she referred to as "those things," but she had no grid for deliverance from them. We exchanged information, and over the next year or two, she would contact me out of the blue and invite me into her counseling sessions to help. God continued to provide opportunities to do deliverance from "those things."

I would continue praying over my mall for seven years, and I saw some amazing miracles. Healings, deliverance, angelic assistance, and joy were common. All the stores were filled, and if a store closed, another one quickly took its place. God was using it for my training ground! You can do the same thing: Select a local store that you frequent and start praying over the store, blessing the business and being open and available for divine encounters.

LEARNINGS

Lesson 1: Carrying the Presence of the Lord

God was teaching me that I carry His presence wherever I go and can impact the environment and those around me with the Holy Spirit, which is always living in me and resting upon me. This awareness is key to walking in a life of healing and miracles.

The book of Luke states, "When all the people were being baptized, Jesus was baptized too. And as He was praying heaven was opened, and the Holy Spirit descended upon Him in bodily form like a dove. And a voice came from heaven, 'You are my Son, whom I love; with you, I am well pleased." (Luke 3:21 (NIV)) The dove representing the Holy Spirit rested upon Jesus and, in other translations, remained there. I find it interesting that immediately after this event, Jesus began His public ministry, which continued for three years.

Lesson 2: Time and Awareness

Committing to this work, I learned, meant being available to the Holy Spirit and being willing to give God my time, whether I was walking the mall or doing something else. I made the conscious decision that He could interrupt my life at any time to touch people around me, and I anticipated His next move.

I also learned to have an awareness for what is going on around me. When I was not at the mall, I set aside time to pray and look for divine encounters. When they came up, I took the needed time for God to demonstrate His love to those around me.

Acts 10:38 (NKJV) states, "how God anointed Jesus of Nazareth with the Holy Spirit and with power, who went about doing good and healing all who were oppressed by the devil for God was with Him." As Jesus was going about His days, He was aware of the people around Him and engaged in loving them. The Holy Spirit rested on Jesus and anointed Him to impact their lives so that they could experience God and His love.

I too am an agent of God's blessing to people and businesses so others can experience His enduring love for them. Bringing the Holy Spirit with me in my daily life allows God to reach those in our community, stores, and businesses. You too can walk with an expectation and an awareness of the Holy Spirit being on you. He wants to work through you to touch people's lives and set them free.

Lesson 3: Be Open and Available

It was during my encounters at the mall that I first learned I can hear His voice leading me to divine encounters. Again, this occurs through my awareness and my willingness to be available. I can see Holy Spirit highlighting people, and I'll approach them with a word of encouragement or a prayer for healing. As I go into a store, I will ask the Lord if He has something for me to do there beyond fulfilling my own needs.

Matthew 10:7–8 (NIV) describes when Jesus called His disciples and gave them power and authority to heal the sick, cast out demons, and proclaim that the Kingdom of God is near. They saw the sick healed, those oppressed by demons set free, and how people responded to them preaching the Kingdom of God. In Luke 10:17, the disciples were filled with joy and were excited because they saw people's lives transformed and were amazed that even the demons responded to Jesus' name. To this day, even after all I've seen, I find that I too am filled with awe and joy when Holy Spirit touches someone.

All Christians have been invited to participate and be the hands, feet, and voices of Jesus, as, according to 1 Cor 3:9 (NIV), "… we are co-laborers in God's service … " Just like the disciples, we get to participate today.

Testimony 1: Drive-by Prayer

Early in my journey, I kept asking the Lord if I should pray for a person with a physical need (i.e. a brace on any body part) or not. He told me to pray for everyone that had an apparent physical need for healing and I didn't need to ask the question anymore. One day I was running late to church and needed to pick up communion materials. As I was walking quickly out of the store, a gentleman with a knee brace and crutches was walking in. I knew that I needed to pray for him but was running late and didn't have time. As I walked by, I prayed that He would be healed in Jesus' name and, though I said it under my breath, he heard and yelled after me, asking what I said. Thinking he was mad at me, I turned around and told him what I had prayed. He said if I meant it that I needed to come back and pray for him – so I did! God completely healed his knee, and he walked out of the store with no brace on and crutches under his arm. I ended up being late for church and didn't give it another thought. It was totally worth it!

Testimony 2: Headaches

One day I was in a really bad mood. As I headed out to the church, the Lord told me that everyone with a headache I came in contact with that day would be healed. I brushed it off, thinking, *Whatever*, and continued on my way. I stopped by a convenience store to get a fountain drink, and as I was paying the lady behind the counter mentioned that she'd woken up with a really bad headache and now it was gone. Still consumed with my own grumpiness, I ignored it and went on with my day. Later, while in line at Walmart, I overheard two ladies talking. One said that she had had a headache all day and it was gone. This occurred three more times throughout the day! God was teaching me that Christ in me changes the environment. He also can work *in spite of me.*

QUESTIONS:

1. Where do you go in your community frequently that you can adopt (i.e. grocery store, convenience store, gas station, etc.)?
2. Reflect on Luke 17:11–19. How did Jesus impact the life of the person with leprosy?
3. Ask, can God in me change the environment around me? Why or why not?
4. How much time do I spend thinking about whether I should pray or not? What are the roadblocks to stepping out and praying?

CHAPTER 4

REST

*"There is greater rest and solace to be found
in the presence of God for one hour, than
in an eternity of the presence of man."*
– Robert Murray McCheyne

Walking in rest creates an environment that God uses for divine encounters. He invites us to participate in opportunities to minister in ways we never thought we would be able to do. Oftentimes I've found myself feeling like I'm striving and thinking I need to do work for God, or I need to minister to these people. When I am in a place of "have" to, I am functioning in performance and not out of God's rest or peace. Sometimes we get so wrapped up in doing things *for* God that we lose our connection *with* God. When I get in that place, I take a step back to re-establish my relationship with the Lord and start walking from a place of rest.

> **"Walking in rest creates an environment that God uses for divine encounters"**

Ministering from a place of rest is an important and foundational element for having divine encounters led by the Holy Spirit. Over time I have learned to be patient and listen to the Lord as He brings opportunities across my path. The next testimony highlights what God does when we are functioning from a place of rest.

RESTING

One Sunday morning, as I was getting ready for the day, the Lord told me that something was going to happen. Though I didn't know what it was, I had the sense that it was going to be something amazing. God had stirred my anticipation and excitement.

I went to church, keeping my eyes and ears open … and nothing happened. Afterward, we attended a friend's wedding, and I had the opportunity to share encouragement and some prophetic words with several people. Yet I felt like there was still something that the Lord wanted to do.

That night, I was returning to church, as we were having a guest speaker. I had some time between the wedding and the church service and, thinking about the encounters at "my mall," I decided to go to a nearby mall. I figured I'd go see if God had something there that He wanted to do, if there was an opportunity for me to demonstrate His kingdom and minister.

While at the mall, I did my best to pay attention and look for opportunities. As I saw people, I asked Holy Spirit if He wanted me to pray for this person or that person. I took opportunities to pray for half a dozen people I felt the Lord was leading me to, and though I didn't experience a miracle of any kind, I remained faithful and was able to bless and encourage several people.

As I walked through the mall, I spoke with the Lord, expressing that I hadn't seen the "something" that He'd promised earlier in the day. After looking, making myself available, and praying for some people, I decided to sit down in one of the overstuffed chairs at the mall.

The next thing I knew, somebody was touching my shoulder. Tired from church, a wedding, looking for opportunities, praying, and giving prophetic words to people, I had fallen asleep!

I woke up to a priest, wearing his robe and collar, along with a man and a girl who looked to be about twelve years old. I'm sure my face showed my surprise as the priest explained that the man and his daughter were from Costa Rica. I was thinking that this might be the divine encounter God had for me, that He had brought them right to me as I slept.

As the man and his daughter spoke only Spanish, the priest served as our translator. Through him, the father shared that his daughter had fallen when she was climbing a tree and broke her leg. Due to the fact that they were nowhere near a medical facility, the severely injured leg had not healed properly and left her unable to walk.

THE DREAM

The dad proceeded to tell me that the Lord had given him a dream the night before. In the dream, he saw a person wearing a shirt with green leaves sleeping in a mall. He knew in the dream that if he went up to that person, that person would pray for his daughter, and she would be healed.

As I was listening to him describe the dream, I was astounded at how God had been working behind the scenes to set up this divine encounter. Like me, the man had woken up that morning knowing that God wanted to do something amazing. From the dream, he knew he needed to go to this specific mall; he also knew exactly what I looked like and what I was going to be wearing. He knew that his daughter would be healed. At mass that morning, he had shared his dream and convinced the priest to come with him to find me. They had been walking around the mall for hours, looking for the man in the shirt with green leaves.

As he shared this dream with me, I could feel the father's love for his daughter. I could feel the presence of the Lord building and that the Holy Spirit was beginning to brew and His power beginning to increase. It was so intense that at one point I wondered if I could handle it. I knew something amazing was about to happen!

We shifted from talking to praying. I laid my hands on the daughter's crippled leg, and the dad laid hands on her shoulders. Immediately, I could feel things begin to shift beneath my hand; I could hear and see it as bones were reshaped and lengthened. When the movement ended, I was shocked and amazed to see a completely healthy leg that matched the other. Though I had expected God to heal the girl, I never imagined something like this!

The girl jumped out of the wheelchair, walking at first, then running around in circles with the biggest smile on her face. The priest was smiling. Her father and I cried tears of joy and celebration of what the Lord had done!

LEARNINGS

Lesson 1: Persistence and Anticipation

I knew it wasn't my faith that had healed the girl's leg, but the faith and persistence of her father. This miracle reminds me of the paralytic in the gospel (Matthew 9:1–8, NIV), who was brought to Jesus on a mat. When his friends saw the large crowd, they dropped him through the ceiling at Jesus's feet. Jesus forgave the man's sins, healed him, and told him to pick up his mat and walk. It wasn't the man's faith; it was the faith and persistence of his friends that brought him to Jesus to be healed.

Throughout that day, I was persistent in seeking the Lord for the divine encounter. The dad was persistent in convincing the priest to bring him to the mall so his daughter could be healed. I anticipated something would happen because God is true to His Word, and He'd told me something would happen.

In Luke, chapter 19:1–10 (NIV), Zacchaeus, the tax collector in Jericho, heard that Jesus was coming his way. Wanting to see Him, Zacchaeus climbed into a sycamore tree to catch a glimpse of Jesus as he passed by. Jesus noticed Zacchaeus in the tree and invited him to share a meal. Zacchaeus had been rewarded for his persistent pursuit of Jesus.

Another example of persistence in the Bible can be found in Luke 18:1–8 (NIV). A widow needed something from the king and was persistent in her pursuit by coming before him over and over again. Finally, the king granted her request because of her persistence. As you step into supernatural encounters, you may need to be persistent even when you don't see anything happening.

Lesson 2: Functioning from a Place of Rest

As I have learned to rest in God with both expectation and internal peace, He has moved and lives were touched in amazing ways. God doesn't want us to be anxious, force things to happen, or strive in our own strength. I believe that He is always at work and our part is to look for opportunities to join Him.

Psalm 46:10 (NIV) states, "He says, 'Be still, and know that I am God; I will be exalted among the nations, I will be exalted in the earth.'" When we are at rest and we function out of a place of rest, God receives the glory. God also gets the opportunity to reveal Himself to the entire world.

In the book of Matthew it says, "Come to me, all who are weary and burdened, and I will give you rest. Take my yoke upon you and learn from me, for I am gentle and humble in heart, and you will find rest for your souls. For my yoke is easy and my burden is light." Matthew 11:28–30 (NIV) When we are functioning in God's strength and from a place of rest, ministering to people is easy and light. I have learned that there is a sweet spot where I am at peace, trusting God, expecting God to move, and at the same time not stressed, not worrying, or trying to make things happen.

Lesson 3: God is Moving Behind the Scenes

In the above story, the divine encounter was set up by God – I was simply a piece of the puzzle that God was going to insert at just the right time. Even when I was in a bad mood and wondering what might possibly happen, God was working behind the scenes, setting things up, and talking to other people to bring it all together according to His design. I learned to trust the Lord and He will bring me into the picture at the right time.

Zechariah 4:6 (NIV) states, "So he said to me, 'This is the word of the Lord to Zerubbabel: "Not by might, nor by power, but by My Spirit," says the Lord Almighty.'" In this verse, the Lord is talking through the prophet Zechariah to the King of Israel, who was engaged in building the temple after it was destroyed during the Babylonian exile. The prophet was letting the king and the people know that they couldn't do it in their own strength. In other words, "You must trust in my spirit to lead and direct you in order for the temple to be rebuilt."

Again, God is always moving behind the scenes. Sometimes, we just have to wait for His plan to reveal itself. Other times, as I did that day, we simply have to fall asleep!

Testimony 1: Walmart

I was about to leave Walmart when God told me to wait, so I turned away from the exit and instead went to the Subway area to sit down. I had already prayed for someone and wondered what else God had in store. Before long, a lady came up and asked if I was Scott. When I said I was, she shared that I had prayed for her thyroid about a year ago. I didn't recognize her or remember until she pulled out a picture of what she used to look like, then said she'd lost two hundred and sixteen pounds since God healed her thyroid.

Testimony 2: Drive-through Banking

Early in the COVID pandemic, I was asking the Lord how to best minister to people with social distancing and masks. I was at my bank drive-through, and God gave me three words of knowledge: head pain, back pain, and joint pain. After finishing my banking,

I parked my car, got out, and allowed the Lord to lead me to a vehicle; the lady inside, I was told, had a migraine. I went up to her car and asked if I could pray for her headache and sure enough, He healed her! Then the Lord led me to a pickup truck with a gentleman who had back pain due to construction work. I prayed for him, and his back was healed!

Then I went to a Toyota Corolla with an older lady suffering from arthritis. As I laid hands on her, she turned bright red and started sweating. She reported it was really hot and then reported she felt better. I asked her to loop back around and talk to me after she finished at the drive-thru. A little while later, she walked up to my car and stuck her hands in my window, clearly unable to contain her excitement. Her fingers, which had been bent with arthritis, were straight and had totally normal movement.

Testimony 3: Scottish Festival

One weekend I headed to beautiful Estes Park for a men's retreat. I had some time before the event started, so another man, who had also arrived early, and I decided to go into town to a Scottish Festival. There was a log toss going on, and we stopped and chatted with a man who was watching. When we asked if he was going to participate in the competition, he said no, he had hurt his back, so we asked if we could pray for him.

We found a chair for him to sit down on and asked him to put his back against the back of the chair. I held up his legs, and there was at least an inch and a half difference between them. He looked at his legs really funny, like he'd had no idea about the difference in length! There is no better feeling than when the healing happens right before your eyes, and that's exactly what happened with him! The guy looked at me and said, "Did you see that?" I asked what he saw and he said, "My leg shot out even with the other leg. I didn't feel myself move. Do you think God did that?" I had him stand up to see how his back felt. He reported it felt much better but still had a pain in the middle. We asked God to touch his back, and the pain went away. The guy was so excited that he ran out on the field and yelled, "You won't believe what just happened. God healed me!"

One of the other guys looked at him and asked if he thought God would do that for him. He too had something going on with his back. We prayed for him, and he got healed. He said he knew another guy that had something going on and brought him back for prayer, then another, and another. I had never prayed for so many men in skirts! Over the next hour and a half, we saw God heal eleven or twelve people, all with some type of back problem. The other man attending the retreat said he had never had so much fun in his whole life. When we returned to the retreat venue, he told everyone he talked to about what had happened, then he gathered up a group of guys to go back the next day to pray at the Scottish Festival. He'd caught the fire and was lit!

> "*We* prayed for him and he got healed"

QUESTIONS:

1. Describe what it looks like to walk in rest?
2. Reflect on Zacchaeus in Luke 19:1–10. What stands out to you in this story? How does that apply to your life?
3. Do you feel like you need to "perform" to make things happen? Why or why not?

Timing is Everything

"With God, there's always an appointed time for things, and when you put Him first, trust in His timing, and keep the faith, miracles happen!"
– Germany Kent

Recall how in Chapter 4, I needed to be at the mall sleeping in a chair at the exact time the priest, the man and his daughter were there, searching for the person he had seen in his dream. Clearly, timing is critical to be able to connect with the right people to do God's work.

I have learned that it is important to respond right away when I hear God's voice – the implication being that there is a timing element to His request. In the past, I have wrestled with whether I should respond right away or not. If I take too much time to think about it and question why, or think about why I can't do it right now, I can fall out of sync with God's timing and miss the divine encounter altogether. Amazing encounters show up when I respond right away, even when the request feels strange.

GREEN LIGHT

One day I was driving to the gym on a busy road when I very clearly heard the Lord tell me to stop at the next streetlight. Though that was green, I decided to obey and glanced in my rearview mirror to make sure there was no one right behind me. There was, a little way behind me, a pickup truck, but it would have time to move around me.

As I came to a complete stop at the green light, I looked in the rearview again and saw that the pickup truck was now right behind me. The man began to lay on his horn, and I could see him yelling at me. When I didn't move, he pulled up next to me, rolled down his window, and continued to yell, clearly very angry.

I continued to look forward while asking the Lord why I was stopped at the green light. In the next instant, two vehicles went through their red light right in front of us. One vehicle was a semi-truck with a trailer, and one was a very large moving panel truck. If I had not stopped, I thought, I would have been hit by the trucks! After they had gone by, the gentleman next to me stopped honking and yelling and just sat there as if stunned. All of this had happened within a few seconds.

At that point, I felt the leading from the Lord that I could proceed through the light and pull into a nearby parking lot. The pickup followed me. As I drove, I had the sense that this was a divine appointment the Lord had for me, and I asked Him what to do next. I was experiencing a great amount of inner turmoil, almost fear and anxiety, wondering what this guy might do to me. Was he going to yell some more or do something worse? In that moment I didn't really know what God wanted, nor was He telling me what to say to this man. All I knew is that I was pulling into a parking lot and the pickup was following me.

We parked and got out of our vehicles. Clearly still upset, he shared his perspective of what happened. He wondered what was wrong with me and why I stopped at a green light. Then when the vehicles went through the red light, he recognized that if we hadn't stopped, we would have been hit by those vehicles with a good chance of being seriously injured or even killed. He was not sure exactly what to do with the whole situation, but he clearly recognized that something significant had happened. That fact encouraged me.

"WHY DID YOU STOP?"

I told the man that I felt like the Lord had told me to stop, and that I believed God had protected us from a terrible accident. As we began to talk, he made some comments that led me to believe that he was a believer, or at least had some orientation to God. On the other hand, it was clear that his church background didn't include hearing God's voice in his day-to-day life.

As we were chatting, the Lord began to download information about his family and specifically about his son. The word of knowledge included that his son was struggling with an addiction. I asked him if he had a son and he confirmed. I again heard "addiction" from the Lord, within my spirit, but no information about what kind of addiction.

> "*God had protected us from a terrible accident*"

When I asked the man about it, he confirmed that his son was indeed addicted to both drugs and alcohol. Recently the situation had become so bad they had to do an intervention for him and committed him to a rehab program for a period of three weeks. The son had dropped out of school, couldn't hold down a job, and went from one party to the next.

What's worse, after the intervention, he hadn't wanted anything to do with his family, saying, "You cannot control me. You cannot tell me what to do with my life. It's my life. If I want to do this, I'm going to do this. Me and my friends, this is what we do. I am not going to stop doing it." He then told them not to bother picking him up from rehab – which was happening the very next day – as he had asked a friend to get him.

A DAD'S HEART

Obviously, this man was experiencing a great deal of hurt. He and his wife were trying to get help for their son and felt like a door had been slammed in their faces. Just then, God dropped something in my spirit. I shared that I felt like the Lord was saying: "He wants to encounter your son and set him free from his addiction to drugs and alcohol. And as a matter of fact, I feel like the Lord is going to send someone to help your son, specifically angelic assistance."

We prayed that God would intervene for his son and do something supernatural and miraculous, freeing him from the power of addictions and the destructive force of the enemy. We prayed that God would send people, the help of heaven, angelic assistance, whatever is necessary, to accomplish this. When we finished praying, there was a sense that we were done. I handed him my card and said I would love to hear what transpired, then we went our separate ways.

THE REST OF THE STORY

Less than twenty-four hours later, the man called me. While his son was waiting for his friend to pick him up from rehab, a stranger walked up to him and literally blocked him from walking toward the area where he would meet his friend. The stranger asked if he wanted to be free from his addiction to drugs and alcohol. The son said, "I don't know," but as he turned to walk away, the person was again right in front of him! This time, when asked again if he wanted to be free, the son thought, *No, I don't want to.* Yet somehow, what came out of his mouth was, "Yes, I want to be free."

The person touched him, and instantly "something" left. He described it as an evil demonic influence that literally left his body. And when it left his body, he expressed that he had no desire for drugs or alcohol and no desire to meet with his friend and party. He turned back to the person and realized they had disappeared! That's when he realized that the stranger was actually an angel.

When his friend showed up, the son got into the car and said he'd just like to go home, rather than the party they'd planned to attend. The man told me that his son arrived at the house a completely different person from the one who had left! After apologizing to his parents, then telling them about the encounter, he said he wanted to recommit his life to the Lord. The family celebrated all God had done – as did I! God demonstrated His love by protecting his father and me from an accident and setting this son free from addictions and reconciling him to his family. And it simply started with stopping at a green light....

LEARNINGS

Lesson 1: Hearing and Obeying

The Scripture that came to mind after the encounter was Acts 10:38 (NIV): "How God anointed Jesus of Nazareth with the Holy Spirit and power, and how he went around doing good and healing all who were under the power of the devil, because God was with him." Anointed by the Holy Spirit in power, Jesus went about healing the sick, raising the dead, and delivering people from evil spirits. I had the opportunity to believe, pray, and expect God to do something supernatural for the man's son.
Again, I have learned that when I hear God's voice, I need to quickly obey – and be confident in what I'm hearing. If I hadn't, things would have turned out very different for both me and that man. John 10 tells us that we are sheep and He is our shepherd. "... and sheep follow him, for they know his voice. Yet they will by no means follow a stranger, but flee from him, for they do not know the voice of strangers." (John 10: 4b–5 (NKJV)) We need to develop the skills of hearing and knowing that the Lord is speaking. I will do exactly what He says to do, when He says it, because sometimes it's a matter of my own safety. We can always ask the Lord questions about it later, after we've been obedient and we know we've heard His voice.

We see Paul responding this way in Acts 16:9–10 (NIV). Paul had a vision of a man in Macedonia, standing and begging him to travel there and help. Being the obedient man he was, Paul left for Macedonia with his companions, concluding that God had called them to preach the gospel there. This example is just one of many where people throughout the Scriptures heard God speak to them, and it is still happening today. When we hear, feel, or see the Lord's leading, we need to say yes, respond, and recognize that it is time to do exactly what He has told us to do.

Another example can be found in Luke 17: 11 (NIV). This is the story where ten lepers came to Jesus and cried out for Him to have pity on them and heal them. Jesus told them to go and show themselves to the priests. On their way to the temple, they were completely cleansed of the disease – all because they had responded to Jesus's command.

Another Biblical example is in the Gospel of John Chapter 21, where the disciples had spent the entire night fishing and hadn't caught anything. When morning came, Jesus was standing on the shore. "Friends," He asked them, "do you have any fish?" When they said no, He replied, "Throw your net on the right side of the boat and you will find some." And when they did, they were unable to haul in the net because they had caught so many fish. Once again, Jesus told the disciples exactly what to do. He told them to put their nets in a specific place. When they did so, they had more fish than they could get into the boat. They were obedient to the Lord. They were faithful to what God told them to do. Peter, James, and John were able to experience the promise and the provision that God had for them because of their immediate obedience.

"GOD'S TIMING IS PERFECT"

Lesson 2: God's Timing Is Perfect

I have learned that God's timing is perfect. He knows when things are set up just right. He knows when it's time to step in and do something. Sometimes we must wait for that perfect timing and at times it's right away. Either way, He will direct us.

In the Gospel of John, Chapter 11 (TPT), when Lazarus becomes sick to the point of death, Jesus declares, "This sickness will not end in death for Lazarus, but will bring glory and praise to God. This will reveal the greatness of the Son of God by what takes place. Now, even though Jesus loved Mary, Martha, and Lazarus, He remained where He was for two more days. Finally, on the third day He said to his disciples, 'Come. It's time to go to Bethany.'" (John 11:4–7 (TPT))

There are several things in this passage that are interesting, the main one being the timing. The sisters wanted Jesus to come right away to heal Lazarus before he died, but Jesus knew that God had a different timetable and plan. God was going to use this circumstance to show and reveal who Jesus was. God's timing was to wait until Lazarus had already died, until he was buried and had been in the tomb for several days. When Jesus showed up, He called Lazarus by his name and Lazarus came out of the tomb! So often, I think the challenge for us is that we think the timing has to be "right now" or something has to be a particular way. We have to trust that God will show us the right timing and that it will be perfect.

Lesson 3: Things Are Not as They Appear

Sometimes what appears to be happening on the surface isn't what is really going on. The gentleman in the truck was upset that I had stopped at the green light, but there were other things in his life that were impacting his response to me. His anger was covering up hurt and concern for his son. People often put up defenses or have a big reaction because of what's going on in their lives. Looking beyond a person's initial reaction can give us insight into their experiences and heart.

We need to recognize that even when things don't seem like they're going exactly the way we think they will or should, there might be an opportunity for a divine encounter. In this situation, God had me pull over and talk with the gentleman, then provided a word of knowledge that changed the course of the conversation.

When Jesus came across the woman who was caught in adultery, the Pharisees and the crowd were ready to stone her. Everyone was anxious and upset, but Jesus didn't get distracted by the emotion in the air and started calmly drawing in the sand. One by one, her accusers left, and Jesus forgave her and sent her on her way. It appeared to be an obvious outcome (stoning the adulterous woman), but Jesus stepped in and changed the environment. There may be times when God has you stay in a situation that might feel uncomfortable and gives you what you need to change the environment, thus changing the outcome. Lean on the Holy Spirit in these situations, respecting and honoring those you are ministering to and pressing through when He asks. He is good and will let you know.

Testimony 1: Healing

In December 2021, I headed for the steam room of my gym after a workout. It was crowded, so I stood by the door, thinking I'd wait a bit. Instead, in less than a minute, all but one person left the steam room. My awareness was cued, and I wondered if the Lord might be setting up a divine encounter.

The man who remained started a conversation with me and alluded to the fact that he might be a believer. I asked him if he was a Christian, and he confirmed he was, so I told him I was writing a book and shared some of the testimonies I was putting in it. He then told me he had played competitive tennis for a long time, resulting in injuries to his elbows, one shoulder, and an ankle that continued to give him problems.

Indeed, the injured ankle was swollen to twice the size of the other. As always, I asked if I could pray for him, and he agreed. I prayed for his shoulder, elbows, and ankles. When I was done, I asked him to test out each one. His shoulder was the most injured, and immediately he realized the pain was gone and that he could do things he couldn't do before. I prayed again, and afterward he had full range of motion in his shoulder – again, without pain.

As he was testing out his shoulder, he realized that the elbow on the same side wasn't hurting either. He then tested his other elbow and reported it to be a "five out of ten" on the pain scale; his ankle was still swollen. We prayed again and noticed a dramatic shift in the size of his ankle. When he got up to walk out of the steam room, he reported his ankle was a "two out of ten!" God had completely healed his shoulder and elbow on the same side, along with his ankle and other elbow feeling much better!

Testimony 2: Girl Stuttering at a Gas Station

On the way to church, I heard the Lord say, "Get gas at the Valero gas station." It caught my attention because it is not where I typically get gas. I started to get gas, but the credit card reader rejected my card twice. When I went inside to see what was going on, I found a long line of people with the same issue. The manager said to everyone in line, "Give me a few minutes. I'm gonna go back and reset the computer in the back." While she was gone, people continued to stream in until there were about twelve of us waiting.

A couple of men in the front of the line were getting really irritated. When a worker in her late teens reiterated that we could not use credit cards at the moment, one guy angrily put down a twenty-dollar bill and walked out. When the gas pumps still did not work, he came back even more upset and started cussing at the lady behind the counter.

You could tell the worker was getting anxious because she was stuttering. It made me so sad to watch her trying to calm the guy down but not able to speak out the information. Finally, I'd had enough and walked up to the guy, intending to say that he needed to calm down. Instead, as I tapped him on the shoulder, he suddenly fell to the floor! I was in shock.

Looking up at the young worker, I noticed she was crying. The Lord reminded me of several times I had asked Him about healing neurological issues like stuttering. A testimony says, "Do it again." I realized this was a divine encounter, and so I prayed for the girl.

Right there on the spot, she started talking clearly. Her eyes got huge and then she started crying again, but in a different way. We started talking, and I learned that she had struggled with stuttering her whole life. People around me were also having conversations, and no one checked on the guy who fell to the ground. About four or five minutes later, the manager came back and announced the credit card issue had been fixed. The guy who was on the floor jumped up as quickly as he'd gone down, this time with a completely different demeanor. The first thing out of his mouth was an apology to the girl behind the counter.

Everyone went back out to their cars to pump gas. I asked if the girl had a break coming up, and her manager gave her permission to take one early. I gave her my information and asked her to contact me. She texted me the next day and reported that her speech continued to be totally fluent. She also shared that her family was amazed at what God had done.

QUESTIONS:

1. Why was the timing in the green light story so critical?
2. Read and reflect on the story of Lazarus in Luke 11. Did Jesus feel rushed to go to Bethany? Why or why not?
3. Have there been times in your life when you thought it was a coincidence that something came together at the right time but really could have been the Lord putting all the pieces together?

CHAPTER 6

Is Your Name Al?

*"Will God ever ask you to do something you
are not able to do? The answer is yes – all the time! …
He wants to reveal Himself to a watching world."*
– Henry Blackaby, *Experiencing the Spirit:
The Power of Pentecost Every Day*

STOPPING FOR THE ONE

One Saturday night, I attended a conference called "Stopping for the One" that focused on ministering and evangelism. We were encouraged to take risks and stop for those who need ministry, to be actively engaged in sharing the gospel, praying for the sick, and prophesying over people in public. I was sitting there listening, and suddenly something inside of me stirred. I got uncomfortable and heard, "You need to go; you need to leave this meeting." I thought, *Wow, that feels strange*. The longer I sat there, the more I realized I needed to go. As I began to ask the Lord, I felt another stirring, this time that God had something for me to do. I asked the Holy Spirit, but He wasn't very specific. It was just this nudging, an urging in my heart telling me to leave.

I got up and walked out of the sanctuary, then stood in the lobby for a minute waiting for some direction. The sense that I needed to leave was still there. I thought, *All right, Lord, where do you want me to go and who do you want me to talk to? Where is this divine appointment that you want me to participate in?* Again, I wasn't getting much to go on other than to just leave. It wasn't until I got in my car that I heard the Lord say to go north on Colorado Boulevard. Off I went.

I drove many miles, listening and asking the Lord what He had for me. I drove all the way through a large part of the city, went underneath the highway, and found myself heading out of town. I wasn't getting any further leading from the Holy Spirit, so I just kept driving. Finally, I came around this corner and saw, on my left, a biker bar. That's when I heard the Lord prompt me to go in. As I pulled my Prius into the parking lot full of motorcycles, I thought, *Wow, I am way out of my element. I've never even ridden a motorcycle. This is not my part of town. I don't know anything about bikers or the culture of bikers.* But I had come this far, and the Lord was clear; I wasn't about to stop now.

BIKER BAR

The first thing I realized when I walked inside was that I was the only person dressed in shorts and a golf shirt. Everyone else was wearing leather clothes and leather jackets; they had long hair. They were hanging out, drinking, socializing … and staring at me as I stood at the entrance feeling very out of place. The next thing I know, the Lord began to speak to me: He wanted me to talk to a biker whose name was Al. This was my divine appointment.

I walked toward the back of the bar and saw a table that caught my attention and a biker that I felt like the Holy Spirit was leading me to. There were three guys in their forties or early fifties at the table. All of them had ponytails and beards and were drinking beer and laughing. With no idea what would happen, I just walked up and asked, "By any chance, is there anybody at this table named Al?" It turned out that, yes, Al was sitting on the back side of the table, facing me. Immediately, the Lord gave me a word of knowledge that Al had recently been in an accident. I asked him, "By any chance, have you laid down a motorcycle recently because of an accident?"

The question must have been dictated by the Holy Spirit because I'd never used the term "laid down a bike" before. At the time, I didn't even know what that meant.

Al looked at me kind of funny and said, "Yeah, I did. And who are you? And why are you talking to me?" He just stared at me for a moment, then asked, "Do I know you?"

"I know someone who knows you," I replied.

Well, that piqued his interest enough that he was willing to interact a little bit more. I asked if he had lasting injuries from that accident. He said he did and explained he had broken his hip and his leg in a couple different places. After four surgeries and reconstruction, he now walked with a cane and was in a fair amount of pain all the time. As he was sharing about his injury, I felt the leading of the Holy Spirit to pray for his healing. I asked, in Jesus' name, that God would heal Al's body from the effect of the trauma of this motorcycle accident and that he would restore his hip and take away the pain.

After I had prayed this simple, short prayer, I asked if he was experiencing anything in his body. Al reported that he noticed an immediate decrease in the pain. I asked how much better he was feeling, to which he replied, "Seventy to eighty percent." Excited, I then asked the Lord to heal him one hundred percent. Al was feeling heat in his hip joint and his broken leg. After the second prayer, the heat dissipated, and Al reported that the pain went to zero. I asked him to get up and do something that he couldn't do before. He was a little tentative at first, moving without his cane, then he began to walk around the table and told me his hip was completely healed and that his leg was significantly better as well. The look of amazement on his face was priceless as he continued walking around the table a couple times.

Al asked a few questions and offered to buy me a drink. I know that might sound weird, but I decided to accept the gift and the opportunity God provided me to talk with him. I could tell that Al and his two friends, Mike and JD, were not sure what to do with me. After God healed Al's hip and leg, he started warming up, but Mike and JD continued to stare.

Al indicated that he had grown up in a Christian home with some exposure to church, especially during his teenage years. However, for most of his adult life, he had turned his back on Jesus and had not attended church or identified himself as a believer for many years. The Lord began to speak to me again, prompting me to ask if his son was struggling with alcohol issues. Al looked at me kind of funny, then said I was on to something. Wow! With the Lord's leading, I told him, "The Lord wants to heal your son and set him free from alcoholism." Al was excited about that possibility and called his wife to tell her. He then handed me the phone so I could speak with her. I found out that she had been praying that week for God to touch their son. I prayed with her on the phone for their son, and she was really thankful.

Al continued to be pain-free, even when he moved. He was then very open to hearing about God. I told him that the Lord wanted to show him how much He loves him and that He hasn't forgotten him. I asked if Al was in a place to recommit his life to the Lord, but he wasn't ready so we just continued to talk.

After about thirty to forty-five minutes, JD chimed in with some questions. Mike, however, hadn't said a word; in fact, he had an angry scowl on his face and seemed to become more and more agitated as we spoke about the Lord. I excused myself to use the restroom, and when I returned JD asked if I could pray for his injured fingers. A few minutes later, he was smiling and moving his hands around, completely healed. We continued talking about how God had healed others, and I looked over and saw that Mike was still agitated. Suddenly, he slammed his hand on the table and said, "Who are you anyway?" Then, furious, he stormed out of the bar.

After he left, Al proceeded to tell me that Mike had put drugs in my drink when I was in the bathroom. According to JD, there was enough to knock out a large horse! I had finished the drink and experienced zero effect, which got everyone's attention.

Not only did God heal Al, prophesy about his son's alcohol issues, and heal JD's fingers, He also led me to have some amazing God conversations with them. To top it off, He'd supernaturally protected me from the drugs that were placed in my drink. God is so good and covers us when we step out!

LEARNINGS

Lesson 1: Step by Step

The first lesson is that God leads us one step at a time; sometimes He gives us just one word or command that we need to follow. Over the years, I have learned to respond to what He gives me even if it comes in these incremental steps, as He's always sure to give more direction once I do. By taking one step at a time, we end up at the divine encounter the Lord has prepared.

Proverbs 16:9 is one of several that talks about this concept. It says in a man's heart he plans his course, but the Lord establishes his steps. The Lord will direct the details when our hearts are saying, "Yes, I am willing. Send me."

Proverbs 19:21 says, "Many are the plans of a man's heart, but it is the Lord who directs his steps." Again, the Lord will direct our steps as we are obedient to what He wants us to do. When it comes down to the details, we need to allow God to speak to us and trust Him to give us the details as we go. In this encounter, God guided me one piece at a time. I had to step out and take the risk on each of those individual pieces, not knowing where I would end up or what He wanted. God knew that if He gave me the whole picture, I might not have gone.

I knew I needed to leave the church meeting. Once I got in the car, He told me to go north on Colorado Boulevard. Once I saw the bar, he told me to stop. It wasn't until I got in the bar that He let me know I was going to talk with Al and that God wanted to heal him. Throughout each piece of the encounter, God was faithful to give me the next step. It was a step-by-step process, and I didn't have the whole picture. I responded to God's voice. I was able to demonstrate God's love in a biker bar and participate in a divine appointment with an amazing series of miracles.

Lesson 2: God's Protection

I'm amazed at how good God is at covering our weaknesses when we don't even realize He's doing it. He's protecting us when we are unaware. I learned that God protects me when I am obedient to do what He wants me to do. Even when things could be harmful or dangerous, God intervenes and protects us from anything that can harm us.

We see these promises in the Scriptures as well. One example is found in Mark 16:18 (NKJV), where Jesus says to His disciples, "They will take up serpents; and if they drink anything deadly, it will by no means hurt them; they will lay hands on the sick and they will recover." We also see this in the example of Paul in Acts 28 (NKJV) when he's on the island of Malta. Paul gathered some brush wood for the fire. As he put the wood on it, a deadly viper driven by the heat fastened itself to Paul's hand. Paul shook the snake off and into the fire and suffered no ill effects. God protected him from the viper's poisonous bite. Without God's intervention, he would have died. The Lord used His protection to open up an opportunity to minister to the people on that island. When we step out with God, we can trust Him, depend on Him, and expect Him to watch over us.

> "*God protects me when I am obedient*"

So often, God will use situations like those in the Scriptures to demonstrate His love to those around us. He creates an opportunity for people to hear the good news and receive His love. God supernaturally protected me from the drugs in my drink and gave me the opportunity to minister to Al and JD.

God's goodness was also demonstrated by taking me out of my element and into a situation that I was unfamiliar with, a place where I'd never been and didn't fit in. God told me what to say and what I needed to do. The whole time I had a peace that passed all understanding. It was amazing!

The encounter had unfolded over two hours. When I started that day, I was going to a conference. I had a sense that the Lord had something for a person, and I did – it just turned out to be under very different circumstances than I ever could have imagined.

God wanted to encounter Al that night. He loved him enough to send me to him. He loved him enough to do miraculous things to get his attention and get his family's attention. When I was leaving, Al gave me his phone number. Later, I had an opportunity to pray for his son and meet his wife.

God shows how much He cares for people and that He's aware of what's going on in their lives. The demonstration of His love breaks down barriers and opens their hearts to His love for them.

Lesson 3: Your "Yes" Opens the Door

One of the important lessons to take away from this testimony is that God is looking for people who will say yes when He needs someone to show His love to. He is looking for a willing vessel. He's looking for somebody who will listen and respond when He calls. He's looking for hands and feet in this world that are open to being used by Him.

I was willing to respond and to go where he was leading me, even though I wasn't exactly sure where that was. I said yes. The heart of the person who wants to walk in supernatural encounters has a desire to hear God's voice and say yes when God speaks to them.

Early in my ministry, we were going door to door and passing out Jesus VHS videos (yes, I realize this is dating me a bit). At that time my biggest fear was being physically attacked by someone and, sure enough, one man answered the door and was so angry he literally picked me up and threw me. I got up and thought, *That wasn't as bad as I thought!* From then on, I was willing to do anything that God asked me to do. He had taken away my fear.

We can see this in the calling of the prophet Isaiah. "Then I heard the voice of the Lord saying, 'Whom shall I send. And who will go for us?' And I said, 'Here I am, send me.'" (Isaiah 6:8 (NIV)) This is the heart of a person that God can use for supernatural activity, someone who says, here I am, send me. *You* can be the person that says, "Here I am, send me."

The same spiritual principle can be found in the disciples who responded to Jesus when He called them. We see this in the Gospel of Matthew 4:18–22 (NIV): "As Jesus was walking beside the Sea of Galilee, He saw the two brothers, Simon called Peter and his brother Andrew. They were casting a net into the lake, for they were fishermen. 'Come, follow me,' Jesus said, 'and I will send you out to fish for people.' At once they left their nets and followed Him. Going on from there, He saw two other brothers, James the son of Zebedee and his brother John. They were in the boat with their father Zebedee, preparing their nets. Jesus called them, and immediately they left the boat and their father and followed Him."

God is looking for somebody who will respond with a yes. He can use any of us, if we're willing to give it to Him.

"GOD IS LOOKING FOR SOMEBODY WHO WILL RESPOND WITH A YES"

Testimony 1: Las Vegas

I was leading an outreach in North Las Vegas with a Youth with a Mission Team (YWAM) and the Dream Center. A young lady on our team had a word of knowledge from the Lord – it concerned a man with a physical ailment. The team went to North Las Vegas, comparable to the south side of Chicago or Compton in west LA, to a very sketchy part of town. The team was made up of 4–6 people (instead of the typical two-person team), mostly men, and women are usually discouraged from going.

As we were walking, the young lady noticed six people together in an alley. When she saw the person God highlighted, she walked straight up to him to give him the word of knowledge, and he confirmed he had that very ailment. He was completely healed after she prayed for him and gladly accepted her invitation for him and his group to attend the outreach event that evening. They came, and they were delivered and saved. In the conversation that evening, they revealed she had walked into the middle of a drug deal! God had protected this young woman who had been directed by the Holy Spirit into a potentially very dangerous situation.

Testimony 2: Snow Angel

One snowy day I was driving to Bible college and decided to go a different route due to the icy road conditions. This one wasn't much better, and as I came over a hill, I saw brake lights and what looked to be an accident at the bottom. I quickly but gingerly applied the brake, afraid I was not going to be able to stop. Fortunately I did, but when I looked in my rearview mirror, I saw an SUV barreling over the hill. Just when I thought it would hit me, all of a sudden, the vehicle slid and went into the ditch.

    I got out of my car and went to check on the people in the accident first. One of the cars had a young boy in it, and his mom was talking to the driver of the other vehicle. She asked if I could sit with her son and keep him calm. As I sat next to him and started talking to him, he asked me a bit frantically what happened to the man I hit. He said it several times and suddenly it dawned on me that he must have seen an angel stop my car! We started talking about angels, and he got all excited and ran to his mom to tell her what happened. I then went to check on the person in the ditch. He yelled into his phone, stating he couldn't wait several hours for a tow. The man in the ditch was an abortion doctor. It was Friday, his busiest day of the week. He was unable to work for most of the day due to being in the ditch. God saved the lives of several unborn children that day.

QUESTIONS:

1. How did my saying yes to leave the conference and start driving start me on my journey? Have there been times in your life you said yes to God that led you on an amazing journey?

2. Read and reflect on Proverbs 16:9 about how God orders your steps. Find two or three other Scriptures about God ordering your steps.
3. Can God interrupt your day at any time? What are your biggest challenges to overcome so He may do so?

CHAPTER 7
MANNA FROM HEAVEN

"The size of a challenge should never be measured
by what we have to offer. It will never be enough.
Furthermore, provision is God's responsibility, not ours.
We are merely called to commit what we have –
even if it's no more than a sack lunch."
– Charles R. Swindoll

In God's goodness and love, He heals and He provides for people's physical needs. Just as Jesus turned water into wine thousands of years ago, God is performing miracles today.

> "*In God's goodness and love, He heals and He provides for people's physical needs*"

I was heading to the convenience store one day to get a pop. I had grabbed a dollar and some change to pay for my drink and managed to walk out the door without my wallet. Once I realized it, I decided to keep going as I wasn't going very far. When I pulled up to the convenience store, I noticed that the car next to me was stuffed full of possessions. I noted that there was no room in the car except for the driver's seat.

Inside the store, I saw Judy, an employee I had prayed for and talked with often when I came in for my drink. When I walked up to the counter, she looked me in the eye and said, "You're a pastor, aren't you?" I said I was, and she asked if I would be willing to talk to somebody – a woman, who had come in the evening before. She said was on her way to visit her sister but was out of money and couldn't afford any gas. The staff had let her spend the night in the parking lot.

Though I didn't feel led by the Lord to help, it was an opportunity, so I stepped into it. I thought I'd at least go out and talk to her and maybe help her get some gas so she could get on the road. That's when I remembered that I had forgotten my wallet and I didn't have my credit card or any way to pay for the gas. I wasn't exactly sure what would take place.

THE LADY IN THE VAN

I walked up to her and introduced myself, then said that I'd like to help but only had a dollar and some change to buy a pop. As the words came out of my mouth, I realized I had no human resource to make something happen. I knew if anything was going to happen, God was going to have to do it.

I began to pray internally and ask the Lord what to do. I remembered a time when God had changed a person's dollar into a hundred-dollar bill and decided I would try it. I put my dollar in her hand and suggested we pray. When we were done, I looked at the bill in her hand ... still one dollar. We prayed three times and there was no change. She still had a dollar bill in her hand.

Now I was really wondering what to do. It was one of those points where I thought, *Lord, I need your provision. I need You to make a way where there seems to be no way. I need You to help direct my steps in this.* While I was waiting to hear God's direction, I turned the conversation to find out the history of the woman.

She told me she had lost her job in Utah and had to leave the apartment in which she had been living. Around the same time, she found out that her older sister in Kansas, who had been in pain for years after sustaining an injury, was scheduled for back surgery.

The lady had decided to head to Kansas to care for her sister while she figured out the next steps for herself. She was in the process of driving there from Utah when she found herself at this convenience store and out of money.

As I was talking to her, someone walked up to me out of the blue, a gentleman I didn't know. The guy said, "God told me to give you this money," and he stuck four hundred dollars in my hand. Wow! I had seen so many incredible things over the years, but not this. And God wasn't finished. For the next twenty minutes, seven people randomly walked up to me, giving me cash in varying amounts, as I stood there in complete amazement. When all was said and done, I was holding seven hundred and forty-four dollars!

I was watching the lady's face as this was going on, and it had obviously gotten her attention. Though she had some church background, she was not a believer in Jesus. The money was not something she was expecting or believing for. She was just trying to get to her sister's home. I gave her the money that the people had given me and told her that this was a sign and example of how much God loves her and that He was trying to get her attention.

She made a comment that she wasn't interested in following God but she was very appreciative of the resources. I shared my amazement in the miracle we had just witnessed.

"YOU'RE A LOT LIKE MY SISTER"

The woman said, "You and my sister would get along really well. She believes in miracles too." Remembering she had said that her sister was having back surgery, I asked the woman to call her – I had felt the Lord give the go-head, and I thought I would pray for her physical healing. Sure enough, the sister said she was open for prayer. She was in favor of what we were doing and was expecting that God would touch her.

I prayed for just a few seconds for the Lord to heal her and immediately heard sounds of celebration on the other end of the line. I asked her if there was something going on and she exclaimed,

"There is heat in my back." We continued to pray for three or four more minutes until the heat lifted, then she reported that her pain was completely gone! God is so good.

THE BET

The following week, the sister told her doctor what had happened and that her back was healed. Her primary doctor, who was a believer, suggested another MRI to see if her back really needed the surgery or not. Now, surgeons don't repeat MRI tests, especially if one was done recently and provided the needed information. Plus, this surgeon was not a believer.

The primary care doctor knew this; however, he also knew the surgeon was a gambling man. So he recommended that the sister *tell* the surgeon that she was healed, didn't need surgery, and wanted a test to prove it. He said, "Tell him if the test comes back and you still need surgery, you will pay for the test, but if the test comes back that your back was healed the surgeon needs to pay for it." The surgeon took the bet. Sure enough, the new test revealed that her back was completely healed. The surgeon had no explanation whatsoever about what had happened. She had the evidence of her healing.

This experience opened a series of tours for her to share her testimony in churches and Bible studies, along with opportunities for her to pray for others who were also touched and healed. About two weeks later, after watching all that had happened, the woman I had met in the gas station parking lot gave her life to the Lord. She put her trust in Jesus and was born again.

This was one of those situations where the Lord forced me to believe in ways that I had not encountered before. I didn't have a backup or a way to provide for her. I was completely dependent on Him to provide. I was stretched and was reminded that I never have it all figured out. God always has ways to bring about His plan differently than we've ever experienced before. I'd never had anybody walk up to me and give me money like that before. What an exciting adventure just to walk with the Holy Spirit and see how and what He was doing in the midst of the encounter that He had set up. God just needs a willing vessel. My faith was increased, and I thought, *Wow, God can truly do anything!*

LEARNINGS

Lesson 1: Faith

The first lesson I learned from this is that God will challenge our faith amid these supernatural events. He will push us beyond our comfort zone to step out into areas that we haven't stepped out in before. It reminds me of the story of Isaac in Genesis 22 (NIV). Isaac was the promise for Abraham. Abraham had waited many years for Isaac to be born, then the Lord said to offer Isaac as a sacrifice. Abraham trusted God, and he believed God would provide. Even if Isaac was sacrificed, God could raise him from the dead. I believe that Abraham was confident that God would fulfill His promises to him somehow. God is faithful, and we can trust Him. In the promises He's made to us, even if it's been a long time in coming, we can continue to trust.

Lesson 2: God Makes a Way

Another lesson I learned from this testimony is that God can make a way where there doesn't appear to be one. We see this in Isaiah 43:16–17 (NIV): "This is what the Lord says – he who made a way through the sea, a path through the mighty waters, who drew out the chariots and horses, the army and reinforcements together, and they lay there, never to rise again, extinguished, snuffed out like a wick." God provided a way out as the nation of Israel found themselves being chased by Pharaoh's armies as they left Egypt.

We see God making a way over and over again for the children of Israel as they wandered in the desert. He gave them manna and water in the desert. He provided in ways that they could not provide for themselves. From this, we know we can trust God and He will lead us. He will release heaven's resources in our time of need because He cares for us. He is faithful to His word.

Lesson 3: Jehovah Jireh

God likes to show Himself as a provider for our needs. In the Sermon on the Mount, Jesus talks about how we should not worry about what we should eat or drink, what we should wear, or where we should live because He's aware of these needs. He will provide for us. Jesus gives two examples in Matthew 6:26–29 (NIV): "Look at the birds of the air; they do not sow or reap or store away in barns, and yet your heavenly Father feeds them. Can any one of you by worrying add a single hour to your life? And why do you worry about clothes? See how the flowers of the field grow? They do not labor or spin. Yet I tell you that not even Solomon in all his splendor was dressed like one of these." The takeaway from this is that we need to stop worrying like the world worries about things. We can trust God will take care of us because we're more valuable than flowers and birds to Him. In the story of Isaac, God reveals himself as Jehovah Jireh, which literally means "The Lord will provide." (Genesis 22:14 (NIV)) I have to be honest – it never ceases to amaze me whenever God provides for a need in my life or the life of another. It's one of the coolest things I have the privilege of seeing.

"WHAT A PRIVILEGE IT IS TO CO-LABOR WITH HIM AND TOUCH PEOPLE'S LIVES THROUGH SUPERNATURAL ENCOUNTERS"

This encounter allowed me to grow personally and challenged me in new ways. I was again reminded that God is with me, God cares for me, and God cares for other people. The woman in the vehicle, her sister, and others were profoundly impacted by God's goodness. This is one of those accounts where I walked away and thought, *This is amazing! God is so good.* When I see Him do these kinds of things, I am reminded of how majestic, how awesome, and how big His love really is for people. What a privilege it is to co-labor with Him and touch people's lives through supernatural encounters. I get to be there. I get to see it. I get to be God's hands and feet. I get to hear His voice. I get to exercise my faith. I am so grateful.

Testimony 1: Full Shopping Cart

The first time I saw money show up, I was at Walmart. As I shopped, I kept seeing the same lady, and God prompted me to talk with her. She told me she had no money and that God told her to come to Walmart to do her regular shopping and that He would provide. She showed me that all of her coat and jean pockets were empty, but when we prayed, money showed up in her pockets, enough to pay for all of her groceries.

Testimony 2: Breakfast

I was in North Las Vegas doing an outreach with The Dream Center. We set up for breakfast and had enough food for around fifteen hundred people. As we were serving, the people kept coming, and when we were done and counted how many people we fed, it totaled over three thousand eight hundred! God had multiplied the food so we could feed all the people who needed breakfast that day.

QUESTIONS:

1. In this story of the lady at the gas station, God made a way where there didn't seem to be one. List the ways God provided.
2. Read and reflect on the children of Israel's exit from Egypt and their journey through the desert to the promised land in the book of Exodus. Write down all the ways God provided for them.
3. Trusting in God as our provider can be challenging at times. Remember a time when God provided for you. What are the barriers to trusting God as Jehovah Jireh?

WANT TO HAVE SOME FUN?

> "Life with God is wilder than the wildest roller coaster ride, and safer than your childhood bedroom. It's more thrilling than the greatest adventure, and more delicious than an Italian cappuccino – if you can even believe it."
> – Stephanie May Wilson,
> author of *The Lipstick Gospel*

During the fall of 2019, several weeks went by when I hadn't had any significant encounters. Because of this dry period, I began to hunger and thirst for an opportunity to join what God was doing and see His kingdom come. I had a desire to see someone transformed by His loving touch, for the goodness of God to be put on display and participate in the encounter. I started pressing into God, praying expectantly and desiring to see Him move in miraculous ways.

As this hunger grew for an encounter, I began to pay increasing attention to what was going on around me. For a week, my senses were on high alert, and I was looking for every possible opportunity – at every meeting and appointment I had, and at every stop I made between those meetings, I was on the lookout for something the Lord wanted me to do and wanted me to join with Him in. Nothing seemed to be happening.

On the seventh day, a Saturday morning, I woke up, and felt the Lord speak clearly to me. He asked me a question: "Do you want to have some fun today?" This was language I understood – He was inviting me into an encounter! I was so excited that He had talked to me and in a way I understood. I had a huge smile on my face all morning. My heart was full of anticipation.

As I was getting ready to leave the house, the Lord began to speak to me again, saying that there was someplace He wanted to take me. I followed His direction and drove for about twenty minutes. Eventually, Holy Spirit had me get off the highway and gave me an image of a van. I drove along the side road until I saw the van at a gas station/convenience store. I pulled into the parking lot and noticed the minivan had a family in it.

"My heart was full of anticipation"

The Lord confirmed that this was the divine encounter I was looking for, so I walked up to the van door on the driver's side. In the vehicle were a young man, his wife, and three children in the backseat (including a newborn baby). The dad rolled down his window, and I introduced myself, then began talking to him about why they were there and what was going on. He told me they were from Wyoming, and their newborn had been brought to Denver Children's Hospital due to complications from birth. The baby had been released from the hospital and they were trying to get home, but they could use some assistance. They had used all their money in order to spend the entire week in Denver and didn't have the money to get back to Wyoming or pay for the prescriptions the newborn needed.

It was obvious I needed to do something about this. I filled up their gas tank and suggested we go to a Walgreens nearby to pick up some medicine that they needed. Sometimes God uses us to meet people's physical needs. As I waited with the dad and the older children inside Walgreens, I learned more about their story. His wife suffered from severe depression and had been on medication since they had been married. She had run out of medication, so I had him order hers as well.

While talking with him, I had noticed the wife staring out the front window with no emotional response. He commented that her depression had gotten worse after the birth of the baby, and that other family members suffered from depression as well. Based on what he had shared, as well as my observation and discernment, I knew something was going on with her and that it may be demonic. I felt led by the Lord to go back to the minivan and talk to her.

THE WIFE

As I went around to her side of the car to say hi and strike up a conversation, she opened the door and stepped out of the vehicle. She had no sooner done so when she dropped to the ground, literally slithered back behind the minivan, and wrapped herself around the back tire! At first, I thought she had slipped but quickly realized I was watching a demonic spirit manifesting. She was moving like a snake, with her tongue going in and out. I believe the presence of the Holy Spirit in me caused the demon to manifest. Holy Spirit then led me to minister to her.

I interacted with her as best I could. The voice that came out of the woman has the tone and pitch of a man's voice – it was the demonic spirit that had a hold on her. Her tongue continued to go in and out of her mouth like a snake's tongue. The spirit told me that I would never get rid of him; he had been there for generations and was causing the depression. She welcomed him, he said, and liked him more than me. It was his right to be there. The demon then threatened to hurt her if I continued to minister to her.

The boasting of the demonic spirit gave me significant spiritual information that I needed for delivering her and setting her free. I knew from the boasting that that demon had a generational right, that it was scared because it was threatening me (which is typically a good sign), that she had made agreements with the spirit of depression, and that it was a familiar spirit.

I quickly completed some spiritual preparation by inviting more of the Holy Spirit's presence, establishing my spiritual authority, and asking the Lord for any spiritual tools I need to minister. Spiritual tools are different methods of deliverance I have learned to deal with the source of the demonic activity (generational agreements, personal agreements, or witchcraft). Establishing spiritual authority means standing in a place of faith, in my identity in Christ, and my knowing God gave *Jesus* all authority, and because of who I am, I have access to the same authority. Once I knew where the demonic spirit came from and how it had claimed a right over her life, I was able to begin to use the authority of Jesus and the finished work of Jesus to break the power of that demonic spirit.

I cut off and broke generational influences, as well as any outside influences. Just like we have connections to the Kingdom of God, demons have connections with the kingdom of darkness that need to be severed so you are only dealing with the demonic influences in the current situation. I exercised my authority by speaking to the demon and commanding him to let me talk directly to the woman. She confessed the vows and agreements she had with the depression and received forgiveness and God's cleansing.

I then asked for her permission to cast the demon out and make them leave. She agreed. The demon made one last-ditch effort to stay and started manifesting again, but based on my authority in Jesus and her permission, it no longer had any legal right to be there and no hold on her. I commanded the demon to leave, which it did – quickly. The wife went limp, so I went over to make sure she was okay.

The wife came out from under the vehicle with a big smile on her face – a completely different person! She explained that she'd suffered from depression for much of her life as a result of a traumatic event. She was also suffering from postpartum depression following the delivery of their child. This was, she added, the first time that she'd felt normal in a very long time.

We sat in the minivan, talking, laughing, and celebrating what God had done. When her husband came out with the older children, he was totally amazed by the change in her. He had refilled her medication, but the events of the last few moments sparked a conversation about whether or not she should continue taking it now that she was completely set free. After some discussion, they decided that when they got back home they'd consult with a medical professional about weaning her off it. It's not always safe to stop a medication cold turkey, and a doctor could support her with next steps.

Our attention then shifted to the newborn in the minivan, and we prayed for complete healing. Watching the Lord ministering to this family was one of the most amazing experiences of my life.

MULTIPLICATION

I was just about finished, and it was time to move on when the Lord put into my thoughts to ask the husband how much money he had on him. He reached into his pocket and pulled out the few dollar bills he had left. I suggested we pray that God provide the money needed to get home and restore what had been spent while they were in Denver. As we began to pray, I felt led to ask him to reach into his other pocket and see if there was any money in there. He assured me that there was no money in that pocket, but I encouraged him to check. When he reached into his pocket, he pulled out a handful of money. It totaled around seventeen hundred dollars, which was a bit more than what they had spent during their time while in Denver taking care of their baby!

The Lord had restored the financial loss from the sickness. The Lord had set the wife free from a demonic spirit that held her in severe depression. The Lord had touched the young child. I had an opportunity to see them on their way back to Wyoming with all the provisions they needed for their family. As they were leaving, the wife told me that I was the nicest man. I was just so excited to have some fun with the Lord and join Him in bringing His kingdom to the Earth!

About a month later, I received a phone call from them. The baby was thriving and growing. The wife was totally off medication and had no more symptoms of depression; she'd also been baptized, either recommitting her life to the Lord or accepting Him as her Lord and Savior. They were also attending church as a family. They were so thankful for our time together – as was I.

LEARNINGS

Lesson 1: Hungering

The first lesson I learned through this encounter was the benefit of hungering and desiring to join God and what He wants to do, knowing He will set things up for us. During that time, God reminded me of how He loves people and desires to see them set free and healed. I found a connection between my pursuit of those things and getting to walk into them. Sometimes we must press in and take some time to pursue God and His kingdom before something happens.

"IF WE RESPOND WITH HUNGER AND PURSUE HIM, THE LORD WILL RESPOND"

According to Matthew 7:7–11 (NIV):

> Ask and it will be given to you, seek and you will find; knock and the door will be opened to you. For everyone who asks receives, the one who seeks finds, and the one who knocks, the door will be opened. Which of you, if your son asks for bread, would give him a stone? Or if he asked for a fish, will give him a snake? If you, then, though you are evil, know how to give good gifts to your children, how much more will your Father in heaven give good gifts to those who ask him!

If we respond with hunger and pursue Him, the Lord will respond. I had desired an opportunity to bring the Kingdom of God to someone that didn't know Him or who needed the encouragement of Him showing up in their circumstances. My pursuit of the encounter, I believe, created the environment in which I was able to step into this amazing, miraculous event with the Lord. I was asking, seeking, and knocking and He – always the good Father – gave me that opportunity.

Lesson 2: God's Timing/Seasons

The second lesson I learned from this encounter concerns God's timing. I would love to see events like this take place daily or even multiple times in a day. Even though I want things to happen all the time, the reality is there have been dry periods or seasons where I didn't see much happen. Sometimes these seasons can be challenging because I can start to wonder if there is something I am doing to interfere; there have even been occasions when I questioned whether God had forgotten me. I wonder if I am not paying attention or doing something that would not allow me to participate in a supernatural encounter. The bottom line is, sometimes the timing is simply out of my hands and I must trust the Lord.

Ephesians 2:10 (NKJV) says, "For we are His workmanship, created in Christ Jesus for good works, which God prepared beforehand that we should walk in them." From this Scripture, I understand that because I am made in His image, He created me to do good works. I am to be His instrument on Earth. It also tells me that He's already prepared the good works ahead of time. I get to trust His timing and that He is setting it up. I know from the Scriptures that as a believer it's not enough to believe that not only *can* He do these things, He wants me to *co-labor with Him* to bring His love and touch lives with healing, deliverance, and miracles.

We are God's hands and feet in this world. James 1:22 (NIV) tells us, "Do not merely listen to the word, and so deceive yourselves. Do what it says." When I hear this Scripture, it reminds me of how our lives are a combination of hearing the truth, receiving His Word, believing His word, and then attaching to it action. He's inviting us to participate. Isn't that amazing?

It may seem to us like things are delayed or even a long time coming. In reality, God is working behind the scenes in situations, putting things together so that at just the right moment all the right pieces are there. When all the pieces are put together, He introduces us to the place of the divine encounter. We see an amazing connection of events that result in someone being healed or delivered.

Lesson 3: Deliverance

A third lesson is that as Christians we have the authority to cast out demons. (Matthew 8:10 (NIV)) Every deliverance is different, but the same principles apply. I listened to God's voice, paid attention to the situation, and pressed in until the wife was set free. The key is to keep your eyes on the Lord and listen to Holy Spirit to let Him guide you.

In 2 Corinthians 10:4–5 (NIV), it says, "The weapons we fight with are not the weapons of the world. On the contrary, they have divine power to demolish strongholds. We demolish arguments and every pretension that sets itself up against the knowledge of God, and we take captive every thought to make it obedient to Christ."

The enemy, in his prideful boasting, gave me key information that enabled me to minister and set the wife free from oppression. Once I knew the entry points and the legal rights that the enemy was using to hold her, I was able to use the weapons of our warfare, to support her in breaking those agreements which took away those rights. The Holy Spirit helped me make the connections, and I was able to take authority, which God has given me in Christ Jesus, over the demon and cast it out and bring the freedom the wife needed.

I doubt the demon even had a clue how much he was helping me in the process. His goal was to intimidate me by manifesting like a snake and declaring that I had no power over him. Demons often use manifesting as a way of creating fear in the situation, and it's one of the first things I deal with, thus allowing me to protect the dignity of the person while the Lord works through me to effect healing.

Again, paying attention to what is going on in the encounter and being in the present with the Holy Spirit is a powerful tool. As you grow and develop this skill, you will be more strategic in navigating supernatural opportunities that God sets up. When entering an encounter, be careful not to bring your own preconceived understandings or notions about how things are going to happen. Preconceptions can distract us from the leading of Holy Spirit and miss how He is leading in that particular moment. You also need to remember that God loves the person and remain aware of how the person is doing throughout the process. The goal is to be able to adjust what you are doing and follow the Holy Spirit's guidance to see the person set free. As you listen to the Holy Spirit, He will give you exactly what you need to demonstrate His goodness and love to people.

Testimony 1: Begging on the Side of the Road

One day I was driving and saw a man panhandling on the side of the road. I had been meditating on Acts 19:12 (NIV), where God's presence was on inanimate objects "so that even handkerchiefs and aprons that had touched him (Paul) were taken to the sick, and their illnesses were cured and evil spirits left them." I now asked for God's presence to be on the only dollar bill I had. I handed it to him, and all of a sudden, the man started manifesting a demonic spirit and grabbed my arm. The light changed, and I pulled away.

I looked in my rearview mirror and saw the man running after my car! I was a bit freaked out and then heard the Lord say to stop at the gas station coming up. Initially, I didn't want to, but I did as He told me. As I put the car in park and got out, I saw that the man was still running toward me. My mind started racing with the possibilities of what could happen. I was afraid he was going to attack me. When he was about ten feet away, things began to change. He stopped running, yelling, and screaming and sat down on the ground, curled up in the fetal position, and began foaming at the mouth! I asked him to look at me, and saw not his gaze, but that of the demonic spirit. I asked the Lord to deliver the man from the demonic spirit, and it left quickly with limited resistance. God's presence totally delivered the man. He came to his right mind and asked why he was there and what happened. I explained what had happened, and he shared that he had been high on drugs and didn't remember anything from the last several days.

Testimony 2: Hot Tub

On March 18, 2021, I was enjoying a soak in the hot tub where I work out. Dave, a fellow member, was there too, and we started talking. He told me he was having trouble sleeping and some anxiety. He was a believer and agreed for me to pray for him, but as soon as I started, he said he felt like he was going to be sick. I knew right away that we might be dealing with something demonic. Dave said he had suffered from depression almost his whole life, then mentioned something that happened to him in junior high school. We prayed for God to minister to that incident and the depression. As we were praying, the demon began to manifest and interact. I quickly took authority over the demonic spirit, casting it out. At first, Dave was not totally aware of what had happened, but he told me he was not feeling sick anymore.

As we talked more, he noticed that he didn't feel anxious and couldn't remember the last time he had been without anxiety. We had a conversation about what God is up to in the world, and after about twenty minutes, Dave said, "This is awesome. I haven't felt this good for years!" We celebrated the fact that God delivered and healed him.

Testimony 3: Special Education Meeting

My wife was in a special education meeting with a parent who was known to be very difficult. During the conversation, the parent's eyes changed, and they turned to my wife and asked, "Why are you here?" In the Spirit, my wife discerned that it was not the person talking, but a demonic spirit. Quickly running through her mind was how to address the real question in the natural without disrupting the meeting. She said that she had authority to be there because this school was under her work assignment. This established her authority in the spiritual realm, and the demon quickly retreated. The meeting continued as if nothing had happened, and in fact, the school team reported that it was the best they'd ever had with this parent.

QUESTIONS:

1. How did God reward my pursuit of Him and my hunger?
2. Read and reflect on Hebrews 11:6. What does God reward?
3. Are you hungry to see God's kingdom here on the earth? If not, what can you do to stir up that hunger?

CHAPTER 9

IDENTITY

"Your identity is firmly anchored in Christ's
accomplishment, not yours; His strength, not yours;
His performance, not yours; His victory, not yours."
– Tullian Tchividjian

WHAT IS IDENTITY?

Everybody has an identity. Our identity is our belief system about ourselves. Identity is the foundation that determines how we function in the world, how we talk to people, how we engage people, and how we carry ourselves. For example, if my identity is that I'm a smart person, I engage people as though I'm a smart person. I have confidence when it comes to knowledge and information. If my identity is that I am physically attractive, then the way I dress and the way I carry myself shows that I believe I'm physically attractive. Our identity can be built on what our parents, friends, or peers have said about us, our educational background, and/or our experiences. Our conclusions and beliefs about ourselves become our identity.

> "Our identity is our belief system about ourselves"

Parents, for example, have a huge influence on a child's growing identity by how they interact or don't interact with the child, by what they say or don't say. Some children are told they are a mistake, dumb, or stupid, which builds an unstable or negative identity. Other children are loved and encouraged and develop a positive identity. It's these kinds of environmental situations or events that shape the identity as they grow.

As Christians, we get to decide whether or not our identity is defined by the world around us or by what God says about us in the Bible. Often there are significant conflicts over these two perspectives. As mentioned, everyone has had experiences in life that shape our identity. If we hear certain things repeatedly, we accept and believe them as true; however, many of those experiences may not define how God sees us and have nothing to do with who we really are.

In order for us as Christians to have our identity based on what God thinks, we must begin to adjust our current identity to what God says about us. The Bible reveals this truth, for example, in 2 Corinthians 5:17 (NKJV), which says, "Therefore, if anyone is in Christ, he is a new creation, old things have passed away; behold, all things have become new." Galatians 6:15 b (NIV) says, "… what counts is the new creation." In other words, we have to learn to begin to identify or accept what the Bible tells us about ourselves.

Developing a biblically-based identity is a lifetime journey. If we are in covenant with Jesus or have accepted Him as our Lord and Savior, then our identity is based on what Jesus has done for us and our relationship with Him. As we believe our identity reflects that we are salt, light, and love, we therefore act in a loving way. We minister in a loving way, and we speak to people in a loving way. This may not come naturally at first, but over time, God's truth permeates our identity and changes us.

Identity is vital to stepping out and interacting with the world through divine encounters. As mentioned above, the basis of that identity can be found in 2 Corinthians 5:17 (NIV). If I am functioning out of the old man, or how I was without God, I function out of performance and religious activity (i.e., trying to get people healed, saved, or delivered) rather than functioning from a place where God loves them and wants to encounter them. My motivation is determined by my identity. If my identity is based on the Scriptures and who God says I am, my motivation will be to love them instead of "fixing them" or doing something to change them. I simply want them to experience who God is through supernatural encounters.

If our identity is not well established according to the Scriptures, we may treat people the way we've been treated. Most of the time, when I engage with people that way, they don't receive what God has for them. People are smart. They pick up on our motivation. People can sense manipulation and performance. It shuts them off from hearing and receiving what God wants for them.

WHY IS THE SUBJECT OF IDENTITY DIFFICULT TO UNDERSTAND?

Simply, it is how we see ourselves. When we see ourselves from our fallen nature, we lack the confidence and ability to navigate how God wants to minister to others. Identity is often difficult for Christians to lay hold of, understand, and begin to function in because we allow our heritage, past, circumstances, and what others have said about us to define that identity. We find ourselves thinking from a "less-than" perspective – that we're going to mess up, we're going to fail, we're going to sin while we're trying to minister to people. When we're constantly worried about making mistakes, we don't carry the life and hope God has for people. We don't have the confidence to represent who God is because we're bringing our own baggage and old ways into the encounter.

When we walk as a new creation and see ourselves as worthy, we can move in divine encounters with confidence and faith while walking with expectation that God wants to heal, deliver, or minister to someone. Faith is defined as hope in things yet unseen. As we lay ahold of what God says about us by faith and start walking in our new identity, it becomes our new reality.

The power of knowing your God-given identity cannot be understated. All we do flows from who we are and how we see ourselves. Our identity matters when it comes to moving with God in divine encounters. When I function out of my human identity, I represent myself to the world. When my identity is in Christ, I begin to move the way Christ moved in love, and I become an example of Christ to the world.

SELF-IMAGE

Our self-image is the way we see our identity. It impacts, and is shaped by, our beliefs. Once we've accepted our identity based on what Jesus said about us in the Bible, then we begin to develop a belief system based on who God says we are. From that belief system, we develop thinking patterns and ways to process the world around us, which also changes the way we act and function in the world. Through our actions, the world around us sees who we really are and is impacted by it.

MY IDENTITY IN CHRIST

The following are practical steps that you can take to build your identity in Christ Jesus, according to what the Bible tells us, and begin to walk in the supernatural.

1. Make or find a list of what the Scriptures say about us as believers. I call it the "In Christ" list, and it includes such things as I am loved, I am forgiven in Christ, I am adopted into his family, I am a son/daughter, and I am the righteousness of God in Christ. You can bullet the list to make it easy to read, remember, remind, and speak over yourself.
2. Make the "In Christ" list into declarations you say every day, out loud. Declarations are an excellent way of establishing truth and changing our belief system. The Bible tells us that faith

comes by hearing the Word of God. We are literally building our faith when we declare the Scriptures about who we are in Christ over our lives. God did not think the world into existence. He *spoke* the world into existence. In the same way, when we speak declarations over our lives we create new beliefs based on the Word of God.

3. Stop the negative self-talk and speak, "This is who I am." We renew our minds over time with God's truth. We root out the lies we have believed (i.e., I am a failure, God isn't for me, I am worthless, I will never amount to anything, I am unlovable, and God is ashamed of me) and change them to the truth of how God sees us (i.e., I am deeply loved, I am chosen, I am blameless, I am accepted, I am adopted, I am forgiven, and I am God's workmanship).
4. Walk out your identity in Christ. My end goal is to represent God on the Earth. Jesus told His disciples in Luke 9 to go heal the sick, cleanse the leper, deliver the oppressed, and preach the Kingdom of God.

When we go into the world doing Kingdom activities, our identity in Christ determines how we carry on these activities. For example, the Scripture that tells me that I am the righteousness of God in Christ Jesus – an identity statement. That tells me that when I am engaging with people, I am not doing so in order to please God, be a better Christian, or be more religious. I am interacting with people not because I am performing, but because I am *already* righteous in Christ Jesus. In other words, I'm not trying to get God's approval through the activity that I'm doing. When I'm not performing, I am free to love people the way God wants them to be loved. I'm free to bring the good news of the Kingdom of God to them without some agenda of trying to change them or making them something else.

The word of God tells us in Romans 14:17 (NIV) that, "For the Kingdom of God is not a matter of eating or drinking, but of righteousness, peace and joy in the Holy Spirit. Because anyone who serves Christ in this way is pleasing to God and receives human approval." We don't have to follow specific rules and regulations.

In the Holy Spirit, we can function from a place of righteousness, peace, and joy when we are ministering to people.

Living according to our identity in Christ is an ongoing process of renewing our minds. Some days, you may recognize that you are functioning out of old mindsets and old ways. When that happens, I pull out my "In Christ" list and speak it over my life. I find the more I focus on what God says about me, the quicker my mind is refreshed and realigned. Over time, what God says about me shifts from my head to a truth I live out every day.

Again, our identity becomes the foundation of what we do, how we make decisions, and how we interact with people around us. Aligning our identity to how God sees us is part of the sanctification process and will continue to be worked out this side of heaven.

> "Our identity becomes the foundation of what we do, how we make decisions, and how we interact with people around us"

"WHO I AM IN CHRIST" DECLARATIONS

I am God's child. (John 1:12) I am Christ's friend. (John 15:15) I belong to God. (1 Corinthians 6:20) I am hidden with Christ in God. (Colossians 3:3) I am born of God, and the evil one cannot touch me. (1 John 5:18) I am blessed in the heavenly realms with every spiritual blessing. (Ephesians 1:3) I am chosen before the creation of the world. (Ephesians 1:4, 11) I am holy and blameless. (Ephesians 1:4) I am adopted as his child. (Ephesians 1:5) I am given God's glorious grace lavishly and without restriction. (Ephesians 1:5,8) I am in Him. (Ephesians 1:7; 1 Corinthians 1:30) I am forgiven. (Ephesians 1:8; Colossians 1:14) I have purpose. (Ephesians 1:9 & 3:11) I have hope. (Ephesians 1:12) I am sealed with the promised Holy Spirit. (Ephesians 1:13) I am a saint. (Ephesians 1:18) I am the salt and light of the earth. (Matthew 5:13–14) I have been chosen and God desires me to bear fruit. (John 15:1,5) I am God's co-worker. (2 Corinthians 6:1) I am alive with Christ. (Ephesians 2:5) I am raised up with Christ. (Ephesians 2:6; Colossians 2:12) I am seated with Christ in the heavenly realms. (Ephesians 2:6) I am God's workmanship. (Ephesians 2:10) I have been brought near to God through Christ's blood. (Ephesians 2:13) I have peace. (Ephesians 2:14) I am secure. (Ephesians 2:20) I am a holy temple. (Ephesians 2:21; 1 Corinthians 6:19) I am a dwelling for the Holy Spirit. (Ephesians 2:22) God's power works through me. (Ephesians 3:7) I can approach God with freedom and confidence. (Ephesians 3:12) I can be kind and compassionate to others. (Ephesians 4:32) I can forgive others. (Ephesians 4:32) I am a light to others and can exhibit goodness, righteousness, and truth. (Ephesians 5:8–9) I can understand what God's will is. (Ephesians 5:17) I can give thanks for everything. (Ephesians 5:20) I can be strong. (Ephesians 6:10) I have God's power. (Ephesians 6:10) I am not alone. (Hebrews 13:5) I am growing. (Colossians 2:7) I am His disciple. (John 13:15) I possess the mind of Christ. (I Corinthians 2:16) I am promised a full life. (John 10:10) I am victorious. (I John 5:4) I am chosen and dearly loved. (Colossians 3:12) I am blameless. (I Corinthians 1:8) I am set free. (Romans 8:2; John 8:32) I am crucified with Christ. (Galatians 2:20) I am a light in the world. (Matthew 5:14) I am more than a conqueror. (Romans 8:37) I am the righteousness of God. (2 Corinthians 5:21) I am safe. (I John 5:18)

Ephesians 2:13–14 (NIV) tells us to "Remember that at that time you were separate from Christ, excluded from citizenship in Israel and foreigners to the covenants of the promise, without hope and without God in the world. But now in Christ Jesus you who once were far away have been brought near by the blood of Christ." Before we knew Christ, we had an identity based on our fallen nature/human nature/out of our flesh. Jesus brought us near to God through His blood shed on the cross and changed us into a new creation.

Ephesians 2:19 tells us, "Consequently, you are no longer foreigners and strangers, but fellow citizens with God's people and also members of His household." In other words, He takes us from being separated from Him, deserving judgment and wrath to adopting us into His family. The good news is we are, as His creations, already part of His family; our identity is found in being His sons and daughters.

God wants to show Himself to the world. God wants to demonstrate His goodness to people who do not know Him. God wants the opportunity to impact people and to touch people in such a way that their lives can be changed. His plan and means for doing so is to send believers – those who are born again, new creations in Christ and accepted in Christ. When we live as one who is in Christ, fully convinced of who we are, we are then free to be instruments for God and demonstrate to the world who Jesus is and what He has done for us.

QUESTIONS:

1. How do I define my identity? Is it by what people say about me, or what God says about me?
2. Read Ephesians 1:3–8 and write down the eight things God says about who you are in Christ. Read them out loud over yourself by saying, "I am … " Was it easy or difficult?
3. Do you believe what the Scriptures say about you? Why or why not?

CHAPTER 10

HOLY SPIRIT

*"It is the Holy Spirit's job to convict,
God's job to judge and my job to love."*
– Billy Graham

I depend on my relationship with Holy Spirit. He is an integral part of my daily life. I remember when I was asking God if I should marry my wife. The Holy Spirit clearly told me not to be afraid to marry her, and I was released to step out and ask her. He gave me an invitation to trust Him and step out. We have been married over thirty years, and our relationship keeps getting sweeter.

> "Through the power of the Holy Spirit, believers are saved, filled, sealed, and sanctified"

The Holy Spirit is one person of the Trinity, along with God the Father and God the Son (Jesus). The Holy Spirit is an instructor who helps us understand the Scriptures. He is a director, leading and guiding us in our daily lives. Through the power of the Holy Spirit, believers are saved, filled, sealed, and sanctified.

Jesus understood that believers would need the Holy Spirit to live, so He instructed His disciples to wait for the Holy Spirit after He ascended to heaven. We see the results of the Holy Spirit's presence in the lives of the disciples, starting in the second chapter of Acts. The Holy Spirit is the only part of the Godhead that lives within us. Holy Spirit has been given to us and rests upon us for the purpose of carrying out what God wants us to do in the world.

What does the Holy Spirit do? (Adapted from "10 Roles of the Holy Spirit in the Life of Christians" by Penny Noyes. (Christianity.com, May 28, 2019))

1. A helper who teaches and reminds
   "But the Advocate, the Holy Spirit, whom the Father will send in my name, will teach you all things and will remind you of everything I have said to you." (John 14:26 (NIV))

2. Convicts the world of sin
   "But very truly I tell you, it is for your good that I am going away. Unless I go away, the Advocate will not come to you; but if I go, I will send Him to you. When He comes, He will prove the world to be in the wrong about sin and righteousness and judgment." (John 16:7–8 (NIV))

3. Fills and dwells in believers
   "Don't you know that you yourselves are God's temple and that God's Spirit dwells in your midst?" (1 Corinthians 3:16 (NIV))

4. Provides revelation, wisdom, and power
   "These are the things God has revealed to us by his Spirit. The Spirit searches all things, even the deep things of God. For who knows a person's thoughts except for their own spirit within them? In the same way, no one knows the thoughts of God except the Spirit of God." (1 Corinthians 2:10–11 (NIV))

5. Guides believers in all truth and what is to come
   "But when He, the Spirit of truth, comes, He will guide you into all the truth. He will not speak on His own; He will speak

only what He hears, and He will tell you what is yet to come." (John 16:13 (NIV))

6. Gives spiritual gifts in the lives of believers for the good of others
"Now to each one the manifestation of the Spirit is given for the common good. To one there is given through the Spirit a message of wisdom, to another a message of knowledge by means of the same Spirit, to another faith by the same Spirit, to another miraculous power, to another prophecy, to another distinguishing between spirits, to another speaking in different kinds of tongues, and to still another the interpretation of tongues. All these are the work of one and the same Spirit, and he distributes them to each one, just as he determines." (1 Corinthians 12:7–11 (NIV))

7. The seal or legal signature confirming the believer's adoption
"And you also were included in Christ when you heard the message of truth, the gospel of your salvation. When you believed, you were marked in Him with a seal, the promised Holy Spirit." (Ephesians 1:13 (NIV))

8. Strengthens believers and intercedes
"In the same way, the Spirit helps us in our weakness. We do not know what we ought to pray for, but the Spirit himself intercedes for us through wordless groans. And he who searches our hearts knows the mind of the Spirit because the Spirit intercedes for God's people in accordance with the will of God." (Romans 8:26–27 (NIV))

9. Gives believers eternal life
"But if Christ is in you, then even though your body is subject to death because of sin, the Spirit gives life because of righteousness. And if the Spirit of Him who raised Jesus from the dead is living in you, He who raised Christ from the dead will also give life to your mortal bodies because of His Spirit who lives in you." (Romans 8:10–11)

10. Sanctifies and enables believers to bear good fruit (Galatians 5:16–21 (NIV) and Galatians 5:22–25 (NIV)).

HOW HOLY SPIRIT OPERATES

Holy Spirit has been given to us for two reasons – first, for our own personal benefit and lives within us; and, second, for the world and He is upon us. Bill Johnson says in his book *Manifesto for a Normal Christian Life*, "We have been given the privilege to host this presence. The Holy Spirit is in me for my sake but He is upon me for yours."

Holy Spirit in Me

When you receive Jesus Christ as your Lord and Savior, the Holy Spirit takes up residence in you. Because I am in Christ, the Holy Spirit is in me for my own personal benefit to seal me and keep me until the day of redemption. Ephesians 4:30(NIV) tells us, "And do not grieve the Holy Spirit of God, with whom you were sealed for the day of redemption." The Holy Spirit is my counselor and explains the Scriptures to me (John 16:13). The gift of tongues. or personal prayer language, is to edify myself. Medical research has also documented parts of the brain that are only active when speaking in tongues, and that part of the brain releases beneficial chemicals into the body for healing and health. Scripture talks about when I pray in the Spirit, I edify myself (I Corinthians 14:4). Holy Spirit convicts me of sin and brings me to repentance. All are activities of the Holy Spirit in me, for my benefit.

"THE HOLY SPIRIT IS ON US FOR THE SAKE OF THE WORLD"

Holy Spirit on Me

The Holy Spirit is on us for the sake of the world. Throughout the Gospel of Luke, he references the Holy Spirit resting on Jesus.

Luke's version of Jesus' baptism says that a dove descended on and rested on Him. As mentioned earlier, Luke 3:21–22 (NIV) says, "When all the people were being baptized, Jesus was baptized too. And as He was praying, heaven was opened, and the Holy Spirit descended on him in bodily form like a dove. And a voice came from heaven: 'You are My Son, whom I love; with you I am well pleased.' From that moment, with the Holy Spirit upon him, Jesus did public ministry."

In Acts, Jesus tells the disciples that He wants them to wait in the upper room until the Holy Spirit comes upon them. Once this happened, they went out and started telling people about Jesus. Up until that point, the disciples were already saved and had the Holy Spirit within, now the Holy Spirit *came upon them* in the same way He had come upon Jesus for the public expression of ministry. When the Holy Spirit comes upon you, you too are given power and authority for public ministry.

PUBLIC MINISTRY

According to Luke 9:1–2 (NIV), "When Jesus had called the twelve together, He gave them power and authority to drive out demons to cure diseases, and He sent them out to proclaim the Kingdom of God and to heal all who are sick." The same is true today, and Jesus gives believers the Holy Spirit as well as power and authority.

In another place, John the Baptist was in prison and having doubts. He sent his disciples to go to Jesus and asked if Jesus was the Messiah. Jesus sent them back with a message for John: "The lame walk, the blind see, the deaf hear, and the and the demon-oppressed are set free." Matthew 11:5 (NIV) The reason I think that's important is what Jesus was accomplishing – He was validating who He was. The Holy Spirit on Jesus was doing that activity because that was what it looks like when the Kingdom of God shows up. The same is true today; the demonstration of the Kingdom of God through the power of the Holy Spirit shows the world we are believers and followers of Christ.

1 John 3:8 (TPT) says that Jesus came to destroy the works of the devil. I love that verse because anything the enemy is up to (stealing, killing, or destroying), the Holy Spirit wants to turn around. Acts 10:38 (TPT) is another of my favorites. I read it every morning when it comes up on my phone. "Jesus of Nazareth was anointed by God with the Holy Spirit and with great power. He did wonderful things for others who needed divine healing, all who are under the tyranny of the devil, for God had anointed Him."

Holy Spirit gives believers power to heal every part of a person – physically, emotionally and spiritually. Healing is more than a gift or something God does; it is part of Atonement. Psalm 103:2–3 (NIV) says, "Praise the Lord, my soul, and forget not all His benefits – who forgives all your sins and heals all your diseases." We are fully aware of the forgiveness of sins, but often we forget that He's healed all our sicknesses as well.

Isaiah 53:5 (NIV) prophesies the same thing about Jesus, stating that "by His stripes, we are healed." Jesus' blood was shed for healing spirit, soul, and body. The best picture of healing is that when we get to heaven, our bodies and minds will no longer experience sickness but be whole in every single area. Jesus taught us to pray, "Your kingdom come, Your will be done on earth as it is in heaven." Holy Spirit brings healing, and you get to participate.

One of the great things about the demonstration of Holy Spirit's power, especially through healing, is that it makes it easy to present the gospel. God opens people's hearts by demonstrating His love to them. It's easy to go from "This is how good God is and this is what he's done for you" to "Would you like to know the One that did this for you?"

I love the fact that the message is not just the gospel, it's the Kingdom advancing because the gospel of salvation is a part of the gospel of the Kingdom.

The Gospel is the classic message of salvation and redemption included in the gospel of the Kingdom. The message of the Kingdom is the displacement of everything in this world that is not from God. *Everything.* Daniel had the vision of the god statue Nebuchadnezzar built. The rock, which is the Kingdom of God, destroyed the statue and grew to fill the entire earth. It's seeing this world, free from the grips of the devil and sin. We have a responsibility for whatever time we have on Earth to see the Kingdom of God advance.

MINISTERING WITHOUT HOLY SPIRIT

1. When we minister without the Holy Spirit nothing, or possibly bad things, will happen. Ministry doesn't work because we can't do it on our own. We find ourselves extraordinarily ineffective. People aren't healed or don't respond to the gospel.
2. The focus becomes "all about me." It tends to puff us up and produce a lot of pride. In Acts, there are a bunch of guys watching Paul deliver people from demonic spirits. They saw how he did it and decided they were going to do it the same way. The problem is they didn't have the Holy Spirit. They got mauled by a bunch of demon-possessed people because of it. Wow.
3. When we minister without Holy Spirit, we can function out of manipulation and trying to make something happen on our own. We may have good intentions, but the people we're ministering to may be offended or have a false picture of who God is. Without the Holy Spirit, our interactions with people might hinder future interactions God wants to have with them. I'm not that great on my own. All good things come from the Lord. The critical point is that we are in relational connection with God as we are ministering.

CO-LABORING WITH THE HOLY SPIRIT

The first step is to be filled with the Holy Spirit. Sometimes it is called being baptized in the Holy Spirit. If you have not been filled with the Holy Spirit, I share how you can receive it at the end of this chapter.

Step two is to develop the ability to hear what the Holy Spirit is saying and learn to walk in a close relationship. I learned how to do this by reading the Bible and studying what the disciples did in the book of Acts. I call Acts "the book of experience for walking in the Spirit." This is where you begin to learn about the gifts of the Spirit and the fruit of the Spirit. As you read how the disciples walked in the Holy Spirit, you may begin to realize that walking in the Holy Spirit is a possibility for you too!

We begin to make declarations and expect God to heal people through us, deliver people through us, and preach the gospel through us. Every morning I ask Holy Spirit, "How do we walk together today and what do You want me to do?" I begin to apply the very same things I did with my identity in the application of moving by the Holy Spirit.

Step three is to step out. You will never walk in the gifts of the Spirit or supernatural encounters until you do so. At some point, you're going to have to take a risk and pray for somebody who's sick or do something that gives the opportunity for the Holy Spirit to move. The good news is, once you are filled with the Holy Spirit and He rests on you, you are fully equipped. Now the fun begins!

GIFTS OF THE HOLY SPIRIT

The gifts of the Holy Spirit are found in 1 Corinthians 12 through 14. The gifts of the Spirit are also called the gifts of grace. Grace is defined as unmerited favor. Another part of the definition, which is important, is the empowering to walk in supernatural living. Holy Spirit provides power to believers to do what God's called us to do.

The gifts of the Spirit are distributed as the Holy Spirit desires. If we're connected with the Holy Spirit, we are eligible to function under every single gift found in 1 Corinthians 12 and 14. There might be times when the Holy Spirit gives you multiple gifts during a supernatural encounter. For example, to raise someone from the dead, you need three gifts functioning: faith, miracles, and healing. Some people may feel more comfortable functioning in one specific gift over others. I've functioned in every single one of them multiple times.

It's almost like Christmas Day when the Holy Spirit shows up with His gifts. It then becomes my responsibility to receive the gift and deliver what's inside. We have access to all the gifts as the Holy Spirit brings them.

HOW DO YOU KNOW HE'S BRINGING THE GIFT INTO THE SITUATION?

As I started on my journey, I was able to identify the specific gift as it was happening or as I reflected on what God did. Now, as I listen to Holy Spirit, He will cue me if a particular gift is needed in the divine encounter. At times I see a picture of someone or something. At times I'll receive some information. I watch the person I am ministering to, to see if God is moving. People have reported experiencing heat, electricity, or turning red as God is healing them. For instance, I start getting detailed information about a person, then I approach him or her and present that information for them to confirm. This shows me that God wants to do something for them.

Another scenario is when I get a pain somewhere in my body that wasn't there before. I walk up to someone and ask if that part of their body is hurting and let them know that God wants to heal them.

GIFTS OF THE SPIRIT

The gifts of the Holy Spirit include words of knowledge, words of wisdom, faith, healing, miracles, prophecy, distinguishing between spirits, and speaking in different kinds of tongues/interpretation of tongues. (1 Corinthians 12: 7–11 (NKJV)) In 1 Corinthians 14:1 (NKJV), Paul says, "Pursue love and earnestly desire the spiritual gifts, especially that you may prophesy." The gifts of the Spirit are given to a person for the benefit of others. (1 Corinthians 12:7 (NKJV))

- Words of Knowledge (1 Corinthians 12:8 (NIV))
  Words of knowledge are facts and information that I didn't know before the Holy Spirit gives it to me. The information is about a person such as their name, birthday, something that happened

to them, or where they live or are from. A word of knowledge could be about a physical ailment or disease such as cancer, diabetes, tinnitus, or hypothyroid – with you either "hearing" about the body part or feeling the ailment in your own body that wasn't there before. For example, you are going about your day, and you realize your elbow hurts when you move it. Up to that point, your elbow had no pain.

I have experienced the gift of word of knowledge showing up in several different ways. When I stopped at the green light, the word of knowledge was about the son struggling with addictions. In the testimony where the lady had a full shopping cart of groceries, the word of knowledge was that she had no money to pay for what was in her shopping cart. If I start experiencing back pain, I think, "I don't have anything wrong with my back." It catches my attention, and Holy Spirit then cues me in that what I am feeling in my body is a word of knowledge for someone else.

The other night, I was in a restaurant and my ears started ringing. I don't have such a problem, so I turned around and asked the guy behind me, "Is there any chance you have ringing in your ears?" He did, and I was able to pray for him, and the ringing stopped. Sometimes it's a physical sensation and other times I literally hear the words.

There was a season when I was seeing cartoon word bubbles with words over people's heads. The writing in the bubble would be a word of knowledge. I would see information about the person, like a name, sickness, numbers, or dates. Words of knowledge show up in different ways for different people. The best way I describe it is that I know something about a person I didn't know two minutes or even thirty seconds ago.

- Words of Wisdom (1 Corinthians 12:8 (NIV))
  A word of wisdom is knowing what to do with the information you receive through the other gifts. For example, I receive a word of knowledge or information I didn't know before about a person. The word of wisdom then gives me what I need to minister or do with the word of knowledge. The word of wisdom

may guide you in inviting the person to do something, provide the solution, or give the path you should take to adjust what is taking place.

When Holy Spirit gives wisdom on what to do with another gift, I know the other gift is available. For example, if I have discernment that there's a demonic influence impacting a person, a word of wisdom leads me to pray for deliverance. The question I begin to ask is "How do I pray?" Holy Spirit might provide the name of the demonic spirit or highlight something the demon says, or give me insight on how it's manifesting in the person's life. Let's say there is a demonic influence of fear. Holy Spirit will give me words of wisdom on how to break the demonic spirit's hold over the person's life. It might be a lie the person is believing or a traumatic event that opened the door to fear. Then I know how to pray to set the person free.

Here's another example. You receive a word of knowledge that somebody's back is hurt. Then you get a word of wisdom that tells you to ask the person, "Bend over and touch your toes. You couldn't do that before. Do that as an act of faith." As the person is bending over and touching their toes, God heals them. The word of wisdom gives you the "how" and "what" to do with the word of knowledge.

- Faith (1 Corinthians 12:9 (NIV))
The gift of faith is an increase in knowing and believing something miraculous is going to happen. The gift of faith can give the nudge to step out into the place where we don't normally go. I typically see the gift of faith whenever I am doing something for the first time. I don't know what to expect, and I'm putting myself on the edge. That gift of faith gets me across the edge. It is that extra push that's needed to get to whatever end God wants. Usually, I'll later reflect on the divine encounter and say, "Wow, I would have never done that on my own."

The gift of faith is an inner knowing, a boldness, and a belief stirring up in me. If I'm worried about stepping out and I'm focused on God, it's going to be faith that's pushing me out.

My focus is on what God is up to in the situation. I interpret His nudge as releasing the faith I need in the moment.

- Healing (1 Corinthians 12:9 (NIV))
  The gift of healing by the Holy Spirit is the power of God to correct a physical or a soul injury of some kind, including mental illness. Mental health is our soul side that may have been wounded.

  The gift of healing can function in conjunction with other spiritual gifts. For instance, you get a word of knowledge somebody's got a headache. It makes sense that God would release healing. Sometimes I receive a word of knowledge or see somebody with a brace on their arm. Note to self: that person might need healing. When I see someone with a physical need, I'll ask Holy Spirit if He wants to heal the person. The answer is always yes because He wants to show His goodness and bring His Kingdom to earth. I then pray for the person, and if they are healed, the gift of healing is in the mix. God is awesome!

> "Miracles are any supernatural intervention in a natural event"

- Miracles (1 Corinthians 12:10 (NIV))
  Miracles are any supernatural intervention in a natural event. When people hear the word miracles, their first thought tends to be healing; however, they can apply to any change in the natural world. For instance, commanding weather to change is using the gift of miracles. One time I was watching a severe weather storm on radar and commanded the storm to dissipate and go around us. The radar changed in front of my eyes, and the intensity of the storm decreased, divided, and went to the north and south of our home.

  Any change of things that happen naturally in the world, like walking on water, is the gift of miracles in action. For example, the mention in Chapter 7 of how God brought and multiplied money or when breakfast was multiplied to feed nearly four thousand people would also be considered gifts of miracles. Jesus used the gift of miracles when He fed the five thousand with five loaves and two fish (Matthew 14:13–21, Mark 6:31–44, Luke 9:12–17, and John 6:1–14 (NIV)). These are all examples of a supernatural intervention into a natural situation.

I don't always have the clearest direction when this gift is in operation. Most of the time, I see the gift of miracles activate when I begin to either pray to ask for something different to happen than what's happening in the natural. Many times, the gift of faith operates alongside the gift of miracles. For someone to be raised from the dead, you need the gifts of miracles, healing, and faith – miracles to bring the person back to life; healing so the person doesn't die again; and faith to believe it can happen. The gift of miracles is a bit of a mystery and it becomes obvious when it starts to unfold. I always stand in awe and amazement watching this gift unfold.

- Prophecy (1 Corinthians 12:10 (NIV))
The intent of the gift of prophecy is for encouragement, edification, and building up the person. Prophecy is not identifying what is wrong with the person or embarrassing them by "reading their mail." It's being able to see what amazing things God is putting in them or calling out the gold in them. In some ways, it is calling out the gold in people when they are still in process. For example, God has a purpose for your life. Right now, you are not fulfilling that purpose, and He wants to remind you of how amazing you are. Prophecy always builds up and encourages. New Testament prophecy is for people to find out who they're supposed to be, even at a foundational level, so that God can bring them into the fullness of their identity and calling.

A prophetic word may be something as simple as letting someone know God loves them today, that He cares about their circumstances and what they're going through right now. Prophecy might also remind them of the fact that God's eyes are upon them. You may hear something you think is irrelevant, but it might be the key to touching the person's heart. The easiest way for me to recognize prophecy is when all of a sudden, I have a thought for someone that I didn't have before. It is typically something I don't know about the person, so I know it did not originate with me.

- Discerning of Spirits (1 Corinthians 12:10 (NIV))
Discerning of spirits is the ability to discern and interpret what's going on in the spirit realm, including what God and the enemy are up to. If you are only seeing or sensing the demonic, ask the Lord to open your eyes or senses to what the angels are doing as well. Some people might sense a demonic or angelic presence and then ask Holy Spirit for wisdom on what it means.

I know this gift is in operation when I receive spiritual information, similar to words of knowledge, specifically about what is happening in the spiritual realm. For example, I am out to eat with my family and get a pounding headache that I didn't have before. The gift of word of knowledge gives me information that something physical or in the natural realm is causing the headache, and it needs to be healed. I start paying attention to people around me and ask Holy Spirit who might have a headache.

In the situation above, when the discerning of spirits is operating, I see in the spirit a demonic device, similar to a vise grip, on the head causing the headache. That indicates to me the headache is caused by a spiritual influence of the enemy and discerning of spirits provides facts or information on what is going on in the spiritual realm. The cause in these two examples is different and knowing the cause guides you in how to pray for healing for the person.

The most beneficial place where this gift works for me is when there is an issue of deliverance. I am recognizing that this isn't only a physical ailment that needs to be healed but a demonic influence that may be oppressing them and/or causing the illness. For example, a person experiencing depression might be hearing voices reinforcing that depression. Discerning of spirits will sort out if it is physical or something that requires deliverance or dealing with a spiritual influence.

As mentioned, I know the gift of discerning of spirits is active because I see what angels or demons are doing and how they are using demonic devices or tools in the spiritual realm. For others, Holy Spirit can guide them by giving them information or a sense that something is going on. When you start ministering in this area, you become more in tune with what is happening in the spiritual realm and begin to identify how different demonic spirits operate. Over the years, I have had seasons where Holy Spirit guides me to people who are oppressed by a specific spirit like depression. Holy Spirit teaches me how to set them free from that spiritual influence.

- Discerning of Spirits combined with other gifts
  Once I determine that there's demonic activity going on, I deal with the spiritual influence to eliminate it from the equation. If the person needs some kind of deliverance, that is the first step. The next step might be a word of wisdom or word of knowledge about something the person needs to do to prevent the spiritual influence from returning. It might be revealing a lie they believe and bringing God's truth into the situation, or it might be a generational curse that needs to be broken. The gift of words of wisdom gives instruction to the person of how to change things so they're not being influenced by that any longer. A word of knowledge about something physical that needs to be healed frequently occurs with the discerning of spirits. Once the spiritual influences have been eliminated, healing comes easily.

- Tongues and Interpretation of Tongues (1 Corinthians 12:10 (NIV))
  Tongues is a spiritual language or a human language. The interpretation of the tongues is so people can understand what God is saying. If it's in human language, it will be that of people in the room. If it's a spiritual language, the people in the room will have no idea what's being said, and there needs to be an interpretation. Sometimes one person has the tongue, and another person has the interpretation. Other times the same person has both the tongue and the interpretation.

In Acts 2, the disciples were speaking in tongues, in a known language understood by people from other nations. I have seen this happen overseas where I've been ministering and had a tongue that was in a language that was understood by those present. It is amazing to see this happen and the reaction of those around you.

The purpose of the gift of tongues and interpretation of tongues is getting the attention of the nonbeliever. In Acts 2, when the disciples were prophesying and speaking in other tongues, the people from other nations who heard it were not believers. All of a sudden, they were hearing about the wonders of God in their own language. This gift got their attention and brought to awareness of what God was doing. Indeed, most of the time you see tongues and interpretations, you have nonbelievers present. On the other hand, the purpose may be to give particular attention to something that's going on. To be quite honest, this is probably the gift that I have least experienced, with the exception of those overseas trips on the mission field or on outreaches.

- Speaking in Tongues
  It is appropriate to use tongues if an interpretation is available. Typically you are aware the gift is being used because it comes to you. Sometimes the Holy Spirit will prompt you to open your mouth and another tongue comes out. Other times, Holy Spirit will explicitly tell you there is a tongue and an interpretation. I have heard from others that they received the first syllable and then, as they stepped out and spoke what they heard, the rest of the tongue came.

- Interpretation of Tongues
  Interpretation of tongues comes in two different ways. The first is the literal interpretation (actually, a better term is translation of the tongue), where it is interpreted word for word. The second is when the interpretation relays the concepts in the tongue in the language everyone is speaking. This is the most common. If you use an interpreter to talk to

someone in another language, there are times the interpretation is a similar length as what was initially spoken.

There are other times the interpreter may go on longer because there might not be the same vocabulary or meaning in the other language, so it takes more words to relay the same message. Other times it might be shorter as they have words that summarize a concept with fewer words. Sometimes people get confused and think, *Wait a minute, that person spoke in tongues for a long time, but the interpretation was only a short phrase.* It's important to recognize if it is an interpretation versus a translation.

You can tell that you are getting the interpretation for a tongue once it comes out and you start hearing from the Holy Spirit what is being said in your language. Many times I've heard the tongue released, followed by a pause. This can be very awkward for the speaker because people are wondering what is going on and who will interpret. I often encourage the speaker to relax and describe what is happening while we wait for the interpretation. Sometimes it takes a few moments for the person with the interpretation to recognize they have it. If the person is hesitating, I just encourage them to go with whatever word or phrase they have. At times once they start, the rest comes to them.

I refer to tongues and interpretation as the gift of prophecy. The two parts add up to prophecy in a way that captures people's attention. In a practical way, when tongues and interpretation are released, I get a sense of urgency that God's trying to get something across or He is causing it for the nonbelievers in the room to get their attention.

FILLED WITH THE HOLY SPIRIT

You may be asking, *How do I become filled with the Holy Spirit?* The cool part about that is you do it the exact same way you got saved by faith. You receive it.

I believe the baptism or filling of the Holy Spirit is essential for a Christian to be able to live out and demonstrate the kingdom of God on Earth. The Scripture tells us that we need to be baptized of water and the spirit. Water baptism refers to identifying with the death, burial, and resurrection of Jesus Christ. Specifically, it's a picture of the resurrection. When you go into the water, you identify with death and when you come out, you are resurrected. You are a new creation in Christ Jesus.

BAPTISM OF THE HOLY SPIRIT

The baptism of fire is the baptism of the Spirit. The baptism of the Spirit is the Holy Spirit coming upon the believer in power, bringing gifts and abilities for him or her to minister to the world around us. The baptism or filling of the Holy Spirit is the piece that enables us to live the way God wants us to live in the world.

We see this in Acts 2 Pentecost, when the promise of the Holy Spirit came to the church. In many circles, it is believed that the church was born at Pentecost, when the Holy Spirit came upon the disciples in the upper room. It was so important that even Jesus Himself, both before He died and after He died, told the disciples to wait until the Holy Spirit came upon them.

Jesus said, "I am going to send you what My Father has promised: but stay in the city until you have been clothed with power from on High." Luke 24:49 (NIV) Once the Holy Spirit came upon the disciples, the church was born and expanded, and people began to respond to the message of good news: the gospel message of Jesus Christ.

The next question becomes, *How do I receive the baptism of the Holy Spirit?* The scripture tells us that we are saved by grace through faith when we believe in Jesus's sacrifice and what He has done for us. (Ephesians 2:8–9) The baptism of the Holy Spirit is received the exact same way. By grace through faith we believe that the Holy Spirit has been given to us in power and authority with spiritual gifts. You can pray individually, or with someone, asking the Lord to come upon us to receive the filling of the Holy Spirit.

SAMPLE PRAYER

I receive your gift. Would You come and fill my life to overflowing resting upon me in power, bringing Your gifts and Your anointing so that I can represent the Kingdom of God in whatever area I have influence in. In Jesus name, Amen.

QUESTIONS:

1. How can someone get to know Holy Spirit and how He functions?
2. What spiritual gift does Paul highlight in 1 Corinthians 14:1? What is mentioned first and why is it that important?
3. What spiritual gifts have you functioned in? Which ones do you desire?
4. Which of the Godheads do you know the best? How can you get to know Holy Spirit better?

CHAPTER 11

HEARING AND AWARENESS

"Trust in the Lord with all your heart, and do not lean on your own understanding. In all your ways acknowledge Him and He will direct your paths."
– Proverbs 3:5–6 (**NKJV**)

Did you ever play the telephone game when you were little? The same message was whispered down a line of people yet most of the time, what came out at the end was very different from what was originally said. As kids, we would laugh so hard our stomachs would hurt.

> "*God is amazing and speaks to each of us individually*"

HEARING FROM GOD

Communication with God involves talking and listening just like when you are communicating with someone close to you. God made us with an innate desire to hear from Him, yet a common question is, *How do I hear from God?* God is amazing and speaks to each of us individually. Also, hearing from God and hearing from Holy Spirit are the same thing. God can speak to us about what is going on in the natural as well as spiritually.

Hearing from God can come in parts, like pieces of a puzzle, or even as a gut feeling that something needs to be done. You may get this sense inside of you that God is trying to communicate something or He's trying to interact with you in a particular way. Other times it can be a picture, word, a smell, nature, scripture, dream, vision, or through other people. Sometimes it comes through the most unlikely people, and if we are not paying attention, we can miss it. In the Bible, God even used a donkey to speak to Balaam. (Numbers 22:23–31 (NIV)) Hearing from God can be received in many different ways. There are literally dozens, maybe even hundreds of ways God communicates with us. God can use any of our five senses to speak to us: hearing, seeing, feeling, smelling, and touch.

My wife hears from the Lord through music, songs, and lyrics. Many times God has spoken to me through movies, sharing a particular phrase or scene. For example, there have been times when I needed to be reminded of who I am in God. He led me to *The Lion King*, where the father, Mufasa, reminds Simba that He is not only His son but the King. Another movie God has used is *Moana*. There is a scene where Moana is alone and discouraged and her grandmother reminds her of her true identity. In both cases, the characters were able to accomplish what they were called to because they were reminded of who they really were, just like we need to be reminded that we are sons/daughters of the Most High God.

I love listening to the Lord as He always has good things to say. One time, during worship, He asked if I wanted to see something special. I quickly said yes, and He opened up my eyes and showed me one of His favorite galaxies. He was holding it in the palm of His hand. I can still close my eyes and I am back in that precious moment marveling at God's creation with Him.

Another way we receive communication from God is through spiritual means. God can use Scriptures that we hear or He may bring Scripture to mind as you are going about your day. We can be reminded of spiritual concepts or things that we know God is up to or wants to be doing. You can see this especially through things connected with His name – for instance, Jehovah Jirah, which means "my provider." God may want to use you to be the provider for someone. Jehovah Rapha means "the God who heals." God may highlight someone at a local store who needs healing.

We may hear things that indicate He wants us to talk to somebody who needs prayer. He wants us to bring healing, deliverance, encouragement, or direction. The spiritual components of hearing are translated through our physical senses and often through our spiritual senses as well. Our spiritual senses are discernment of spirits, seeing in the spirit, and hearing what Holy Spirit says. God wants us to hear His voice. He wants us to respond to His voice and believe that He wants to interact with us.

GOD DESIRES TO COMMUNICATE WITH US

The first key is the fact that God wants to speak to us. The Gospel of John Chapter 10 calls God the Good Shepherd. We are the sheep, and as His sheep we hear His voice and we follow no others. Being able to hear God's voice is not specific to a leader, a pastor, a missionary, or somebody who is in a position of leadership. All of His sheep, those who know Him, those who are His kids, His sons and daughters, can hear His voice. He wants to interact with us.

> *"God wants to speak to us"*

People struggle with the idea that God really wants to talk with them. The good news is that He does because He wants to be in relationship with us. He wants to be connected with us. It's impossible to have a relationship without having communication, without exchanging ideas and thoughts with one another. Think about a relationship you have, be it with a friend, parent, spouse, co-worker, or sibling. What would that relationship look like if you didn't communicate with that person? Likely, not too strong, and it will eventually wane and possibly even end.

Marriage relationships are some of the most intimate, therefore communication is especially vital. The more husbands and wives share their hearts, dreams, and concerns with each other, the deeper and closer the relationship grows. When communication is shallow and centers on more surface concepts like daily schedules or the weather, the people grow apart. The regular exchange of words and sharing what's going on and what's being thought of form the relationship and continue to maintain and make it stronger over time.

Just like a marriage relationship, God wants a close relationship with us. The only way that's going to take place is if we engage in communication with Him; thus, hearing Him is an important part of our interaction. Hearing from God is a normal part of Christian living. Through communication, we are led to have the divine encounters and interactions with people around us that He wants to touch.

AWARENESS

The second key to divine encounters is awareness, which has been discussed several times throughout this book. Awareness has two levels – spiritual and physical. We are aware that God wants to talk to us. We know He wants to communicate with us and talks to us in many different ways. The next level of awareness is to be cognizant of what is going on around us. Being aware of what is going on around me hasn't always come naturally; in fact, there are still times when I get caught up in my own thoughts and what is on my schedule or what I need to get done. Then I am reminded to practice being aware of what's going on around me in the natural and in the physical. Over the years, I have gotten better at this. As I am more aware of what is going on around me, God is able to break into my day and show me people close by who need a touch from Him.

Do you see people who have medical devices like a wheelchair, a brace on their leg, neck support, or a sling on their arm? God might want to use you to show them His love. God might want to direct us and speak to us. When we're aware, we can also begin to ask questions and begin to respond to that environment as the Lord directs us. So, for instance, we see a sling on somebody's shoulder. We can ask the Lord, *Do You want me to pray for healing or do You want me to do something else?* As you increase your awareness of what is going on around you, you can talk with the Lord to see what He wants you to do.

As you begin to increase in your awareness of your physical environment, you can then tap into spiritual awareness. Are we connected with the Lord and sensing His closeness? Are we looking to Him? Are we expecting Holy Spirit to talk to us? Are we available to Him? What is the Holy Spirit doing in this environment?

Sometimes God speaks very specifically and sometimes it is more of a general thought. As I have practiced hearing from God and responding quickly to what He says, I receive more specific information like a name or a hurt body part, etc. Other times, I sense the Lord leading me to pray for healing and then someone with a knee brace walks by. Maybe you have the sense that the Holy Spirit wants to do something. Ask, *"What do you want to do?"* Begin to look with your spiritual eyes and see if the Lord is directing you to somebody specific. There may be a circumstance we need to engage in.

Our focus needs to be continually on God. At times He may give you spiritual discernment and reveal what the enemy is doing in a room. Are you discerning a specific demonic spirit or that somebody needs ministry to deal with demonic activity in their lives? Maybe they need some level of deliverance or they need you to take authority over a demonic spirit so they have the opportunity to respond to the Lord. Maybe they need healing of trauma to be set free. God will give you insight and wisdom to bring His Kingdom into the world.

Another area of spiritual awareness is knowing the Lord wants to heal and set people free. The gifts of the Spirit are made available for divine encounter. Our awareness of these spiritual truths and what He has for us will help us engage and will direct us to specific encounters. God uses the two levels of awareness, physical and spiritual, to demonstrate His love for people.

NEXT STEPS

I challenge you over the next few days to be aware as you move through your day. Pay attention to people's facial expressions and what they might be feeling. Identify who is in the room with you. Observe what is going on in the room. Practice observing the physical environment. Is there anybody in the room who has a cast on their arm or a brace on their knee? Next, connect with the Lord and ask Him questions about what is going on in the room, then be still and listen. God is faithful and will speak to you. It is okay if you don't sense something right away. Keep practicing, watching, and listening. Practicing being aware of the physical and spiritual environment sets you up for divine encounters.

QUESTIONS:

1. Do I expect God to speak to me repeatedly and regularly? Am I aware of Him speaking daily?
2. Read John 10:27 out loud and declare it over your life.
3. How does God speak to you? Write down the ways that God has spoken to you in the past.
4. How often do I check my spiritual awareness or check in with Holy Spirit?

Chapter 12

Believing and Acting

*"Trust and obey, for there's no other way.
To be happy in Jesus, but to trust and obey."
– Hymn by John H Sammis, 1887*

We must become far bolder in how we engage the world around us and how we engage our day-to-day lives. Boldness is a picture of what we believe. We will be bold and will pursue things that we are passionate about and believe in.

A belief is faith developed. Once our faith has been developed and established, then we act upon that belief, expecting certain outcomes.

I believe:

- God is good
- God loves people (John 3:16–17)
- God wants to use me to demonstrate His love to the world (Matthew 28:18–20)

These core beliefs lead me to step out and touch people's lives with God's goodness. When we're bold and respond, we know that this is something we believe in. When our beliefs are carried out, we act upon those beliefs.

WHAT SHOULD WE BELIEVE?

According to the Word of God, "So then faith comes by hearing, and hearing by the Word of God." (Romans 10:17 NKJV) The Bible becomes our source, through which we begin to develop our faith that translates into our beliefs. Beliefs translate into our actions and how we engage the world around us. The Scriptures are key to building our beliefs. Read the Bible. Take the promises, the encouragement, and the examples to build your belief.

There are three core areas that I think are essential if we want to step out and become effective in seeing supernatural activity all around us: God wants to demonstrate His love and goodness, God wants to use me, and the world needs to encounter God.

GOD WANTS TO DEMONSTRATE HIS LOVE AND GOODNESS

First, we need to believe that God wants to demonstrate His love to people. Love is His nature and who He is. He wants people to know that He loves them. God is also good, and one of the ways He demonstrates His goodness is through supernatural activity. As mentioned earlier, Acts 10:38 (NKJV) tells us, "how God anointed Jesus of Nazareth with the Holy Spirit and with power, who went about doing good and healing all who were oppressed by the devil, for God was with Him." In the Scripture, we have the example that healing and doing good are connected. Goodness is connected to who He is, His promises, and how He describes Himself. "And we know that in all things God works for the good of those who love him, who have been called according to His purpose." Romans 8:28 (NIV)

GOD WANTS TO USE ME

A second belief is that God wants to use me to demonstrate His goodness and love. He partners with His sons and daughters,

His disciples, His kids, and His church to expand and increase the Kingdom on Earth. What an amazing honor to co-labor with God and see His Kingdom come on the Earth. Our actions demonstrate who God is. He moves through us. We are His hands and feet doing the things He's commanded us to do.

THE WORLD NEEDS GOD

The third belief is that the world is in need of God – it will not change on its own. It needs a clear representation of who God is. Remember the young man who was kicked in the mosh pit? He said, "I knew that if there was a God, He would do things like this (perform miracles)."

We are the salt and light in the world. (Matthew 5:13–16) We are the examples. We are the mouthpiece. We are the witness of who God is on the Earth. It is important that we believe that the world needs God and that it will respond to Him. Jesus said, "And I, when I am lifted up from the earth, I will draw all people to myself." (John 12:32, NIV) The world needs what God has entrusted to us to release. We carry life, hope, and love.

EVERYDAY CHRISTIAN LIVING

I want to dispel the myth that supernatural encounters are only connected to events or specific people. Divine encounters can be a part of our everyday life. Most of the supernatural activity that I've experienced happens in my day-to-day!

Sometimes we talk ourselves out of following the initial nudges the Lord gives us, especially in a time when we're not expecting it. Divine encounters often play out when we are not expecting something to happen or at a time that is not scheduled. Scheduling events and outreach are amazing, and I have seen the Lord move during those times. But the most impactful encounters have come when I am going through my day and God steps in and interrupts.

The best times are when you are just going about your business and God talks to you or points someone out. You respond and He meets you right where you are. The most amazing things the Holy Spirit wants to do are connected to times when we least expect Him to use us. We get to make a choice to respond. In the encounter stopping at the green light, I responded immediately and saw God encounter an entire family.

This highlights the fact that often divine appointments come when we are willing to say yes to Holy Spirit and allow Him to change our schedule. Most of life is not a program, event, or a service. Our lives are comprised of a few events that might take a couple hours a week. That leaves over a hundred and sixty hours a week that we are living our lives meeting people who are not at those events and may not know God. They may be at the grocery stores, buying gasoline, working, at people's houses, going to school events, or at special occasions.

NEXT STEPS

You may be wondering, *Now what?* The last few pages of this book include practical ideas how you too can do what I've talked about in these testimonies. How do we actively engage in seeing God move through us and touch people around us, to see people healed and delivered and saved and set free? Here are practical pieces that have been woven throughout this entire book that I want to highlight:

1. Know that God is with you. I have spent years developing this awareness, which means you can do it too. I developed an expectation and an orientation to life that included knowing I'm the one that God wants to use, just as He wants to partner with all of us to demonstrate His love for the world.
2. Develop a lifestyle where you're aware of what's going on around you. Who are the people that are in your environment? What are they doing? Is there a reason we're all in the same place at

the same time? Are there people in the room who are acting differently from everybody else? I don't want to overlook opportunities that the Holy Spirit has for me.
3. Relate to Holy Spirit. Learn what He does, how He engages us, and what He brings. You can learn about Him by studying the Scriptures, reading other people's relationship with Holy Spirit, and by simply asking Him to show you. Testimonies and talking with others who walk closely with Holy Spirit helped me know who the Holy Spirit is, how He engages with us, how He talks, and what He brings into situations. Study His gifts (I Corinthians 12) and His fruit (Galatians 5:22–23). The book of Acts is a great place to start. Developing intimacy and relationship with the Holy Spirit is a critical element to walking in divine encounters.

> ## "DEVELOPING INTIMACY AND RELATIONSHIP WITH THE HOLY SPIRIT IS A CRITICAL ELEMENT TO WALKING IN DIVINE ENCOUNTERS"

4. Talk with God. He wants to talk to us all the time, every day, probably way more than we imagine. He's using circumstances, situations, Scriptures, dreams, words, music, nature, discernment, and people around us. He's using countless ways to engage with us. You can test if you are hearing God by the fruit that it brings. If it brings life and joy, it is God. If it brings shame, condemnation, and sorrow, it is not God. By learning how to hear and recognize His voice, He can guide you in sharing His goodness and love with others.
5. Take a risk. Open your mouth with what you feel Holy Spirit has given you for the person. Give the person what you've got at that point, even if you don't have everything. Be careful of overthinking as you can easily talk yourself out of it and second guess yourself. It is okay to make mistakes; that is how we learn and grow. Sometimes what I hear doesn't make sense to me, but it is exactly what the person needs. God knows what is going on, and we can trust Him.

QUESTIONS:

1. What is holding me back from stepping out and praying for people or giving them an encouraging word?
2. Read Acts 8:4–8. Are you ready for uncontrollable joy to fill your city? What would it look like?
3. Do I want to be the person God uses to expanding His Kingdom? Am I willing to risk stepping out and respond to God's direction?

Conclusion

God is on the move! He is inviting you into a lifestyle displaying His goodness and love to a lost and dying world. Now is the time to respond. You can do it. I believe this is a unique season in human history where all believers get to participate.

God is enlisting an army and courting a bride – a passionate bride who wants to see the Heavenly Father glorified through people experiencing life-changing encounters with Him. These signs that follow those who believe include healing, miracles, deliverance, and gifts of the Spirit freely flowing. When believers step out in faith it results in people being set free, lives being restored, and wounds being healed emotionally and physically.

> **"We have the privilege of co-laboring with Holy Spirit to see His kingdom released on the Earth"**

It is time to step into a lifestyle of hearing God's voice, to respond in faith, and take the risk to share God's love. We have the privilege of co-laboring with Holy Spirit to see His kingdom released on the Earth. There is no greater joy than seeing people saved and set free from the hold of the enemy.

God has prepared so much more for us – more than we have ever dreamed or imagined. "However, as it is written: What no eye has seen, what no ear has heard, and what no human has conceived, the things God has prepared for those who love Him." (1 Corinthians 2:9 (NIV)) It's time for us to begin to move in things that we have not seen, in things that we haven't even dreamed of yet, that God has set up for us. These include good works.

We bring the kingdom of God by demonstrating how good God is. He is always on the move. We show people that Jesus is real. He is alive. He is always in their corner. He loves them, and He gave His life for us and has extended the invitation of salvation to us that believe. We then become believers that carry and become the world-changers that God intended.

The Holy Spirit in me benefits me and gives me what I need to carry God's goodness into the world. He sealed me unto the day of salvation. He encourages me. He is with me. He is close to me. He brings revelation through the Scripture. He uses the gift of tongues to edify and build me up.

Isn't that amazing? Also in Luke 9, it says Jesus told them they would be doing the same thing that He was. He gave them that authority and power. The Holy Spirit rests upon believers for the purpose of impacting the world. In the same chapter, Jesus sent out the disciples to proclaim the Kingdom of God and heal all who were sick.

The same is true today of believers. In Matthew 28, the Great Commission, it says, "Therefore, go and make disciples of all nations, baptizing them in the name of the Father of the Son and the Holy Spirit, and teaching them to obey everything I have commanded you. And surely, I am with you always, to the very end of the age." (Matthew 28: 19–20 (NIV))

We get to participate in miracles, signs and wonders, and healing the sick. We also know from the Gospel of John 14: 12 (NIV) says, "Very truly I tell you, whoever believes in me will do the works I have been doing, and they will do even greater things than these, because I am going to the Father." Jesus is seated at the right hand of the Father. He is interceding on our behalf. We are in a position to actively engage in God's work. We know from Ephesians 2:10

(NIV), "For we are God's handiwork created in Christ Jesus to do good works which God prepared in advance for us to do."

God promised in Philippians 4:13 (KJV) "I can do all things through Christ who strengthens me." The Passion Translation says it this way, "I know what it means to lack, and I know what it means to experience overwhelming abundance. For I'm trained in the secret of overcoming all things, whether in fullness or in hunger. And I find that the strength of Christ's explosive power infuses me to conquer every difficulty." Philippians 4:12–13 (TPT) Truly, He has given us everything we need.

"IT'S TIME TO WAKE UP. IT'S TIME TO GET UP"

It's time to wake up. It's time to get up. It's time to put action to our thoughts and our beliefs. It's time to do more than just sit in a church service and watch others or hear about what others are doing. It's time for us to take God outside the four walls of the church and bring the Kingdom everywhere we go. It's time for us to believe and take a risk, grow and develop a lifestyle where God could speak to us and use us anytime, anywhere, any way He wants to. Jesus said the fields are ripe to harvest. There's a harvest that needs to be reaped. God is waiting for you to say yes. Are you ready for adventure?

About the Authors

Scott Pearson is a fourth-generation pastor and the senior leader and founder of Bridgeway House Churches. He walks in the prophetic, miracles, signs, and wonders through his daily life. He was the co-founder of the Bridgeway School of Supernatural Ministry in Denver, Colorado.

Scott served on the Board for the Ahka Outreach Center, Orphanage and Apostolic Ministry in Thailand for fifteen years and served on the Board for The Dream Center in Las Vegas, Nevada. He also led outreaches with the Dream Center. Scott teaches at Youth With a Mission bases during Discipleship Training Schools on the Holy Spirit and how to walk in the supernatural. Scott's vision is to raise up revivalists and world-changers in their true identity in Christ so his ceiling becomes their floor.

Lynea Pearson is a joy-filled and prophetic mom, pastor's wife, dancer, and school district special education administrator. She has been a strong supporter to Scott and the church and keeps him organized. She loves to support families and students with disabilities and has for years beginning when she was a speech language pathologist. She leads the worship dance team at Bridgeway Church and mentors young women. She and Scott have two grown children, Hannah and John.

website: scottpearsonministry.com
email: info@scottpearsonministry.com

www.ingramcontent.com/pod-product-compliance
Lightning Source LLC
Chambersburg PA
CBHW070200100426
42743CB00013B/2994